Cambridge Elements

Elements in the Philosophy of Immanuel Kant
edited by
Desmond Hogan
Princeton University
Howard Williams
University of Cardiff
Allen Wood
Indiana University

KANT ON RESPECT
(ACHTUNG)

Jörg Noller
LMU Munich

Shaftesbury Road, Cambridge CB2 8EA, United Kingdom

One Liberty Plaza, 20th Floor, New York, NY 10006, USA

477 Williamstown Road, Port Melbourne, VIC 3207, Australia

314–321, 3rd Floor, Plot 3, Splendor Forum, Jasola District Centre, New Delhi – 110025, India

103 Penang Road, #05–06/07, Visioncrest Commercial, Singapore 238467

Cambridge University Press is part of Cambridge University Press & Assessment, a department of the University of Cambridge.

We share the University's mission to contribute to society through the pursuit of education, learning and research at the highest international levels of excellence.

www.cambridge.org
Information on this title: www.cambridge.org/9781009511056

DOI: 10.1017/9781009511049

© Jörg Noller 2025

This publication is in copyright. Subject to statutory exception and to the provisions of relevant collective licensing agreements, no reproduction of any part may take place without the written permission of Cambridge University Press & Assessment.

When citing this work, please include a reference to the DOI 10.1017/9781009511049

First published 2025

A catalogue record for this publication is available from the British Library

ISBN 978-1-009-51105-6 Hardback
ISBN 978-1-009-51107-0 Paperback
ISSN 2397-9461 (online)
ISSN 2514-3824 (print)

Cambridge University Press & Assessment has no responsibility for the persistence or accuracy of URLs for external or third-party internet websites referred to in this publication and does not guarantee that any content on such websites is, or will remain, accurate or appropriate.

For EU product safety concerns, contact us at Calle de José Abascal, 56, 1°, 28003 Madrid, Spain, or email eugpsr@cambridge.org

Kant on Respect *(Achtung)*

Elements in the Philosophy of Immanuel Kant

DOI: 10.1017/9781009511049
First published online: December 2025

Jörg Noller
LMU Munich
Author for correspondence: Jörg Noller, joerg.noller@lrz.uni-muenchen.de

Abstract: This Element reconstructs Kant's puzzling statements about the moral feeling of respect (*Achtung*), which is "a feeling self-wrought by means of a rational concept and therefore specifically different" from all common feelings (4:401n.). The focus is on the systematic position of respect within the framework of Kant's major works and within the faculties of the human mind. The concept of respect is discussed with regard to (i) the transcendental problem of noumenal causation in Kant's first *Critique*; (ii) the practical problem of moral motivation in Kant's second *Critique*; (iii) the aesthetic problem of feeling and the dynamic sublime in Kant's third *Critique*; and (iv) the problem of moral imputability and education in Kant's *Religion* and *Metaphysics of Morals*. By considering its self-reflective volitional structure, this Element argues for a compatibilist account of the moral feeling of respect, according to which both intellectualist and affectivist interpretations are true.

Keywords: respect, moral feeling, moral motivation, autonomy, moral imputability

© Jörg Noller 2025

ISBNs: 9781009511056 (HB), 9781009511070 (PB), 9781009511049 (OC)
ISSNs: 2397-9461 (online), 2514-3824 (print)

Contents

1 Introduction: The Puzzle of Respect   1

2 Situating Respect: Feeling, Cognition, Will, and Choice   7

3 Distinguishing Respect: Beyond Moral Sense, Compassion, and Love   15

4 Grounding Respect: Beyond Affectivism and Intellectualism   19

5 Reason's Self-Consciousness: The Autonomy of Respect   30

6 Avoiding Self-Conceit: The Impact of Respect   39

7 Feeling Reason: The Phenomenology of Moral Respect   49

8 Cultivating Morality: The Education of Respect   55

9 Conclusion: Solving the Puzzle   64

References   67

1 Introduction: The Puzzle of Respect

Kant considered the problem of rational moral motivation as one of the great questions in practical philosophy. In the introduction to his *Critique of Practical Reason*, Kant raises the question of "whether pure reason of itself alone suffices to determine the will or whether it can be a determining ground of the will only as empirically conditioned" (5:16). In his *Lectures on Ethics*, Kant refers to this problem even more explicitly, stating that "[n]obody can or ever will comprehend how the understanding should have a motivating power; it can admittedly judge, but to give this judgement power so that it becomes a motive able to impel the will to performance of an action – to understand this is the philosophers' stone" (27:1225). Of special importance for his theory of rational moral motivation is Kant's conception of the moral feeling of respect or reverence (*Achtung*).[1] This very feeling can be understood as the "philosopher's stone" that Kant referred to in his *Lectures on Ethics*, and it has been described as "one of the linchpins of Kant's moral theory" (DeWitt 2014, 62) and "one of the most controversial terms in his entire practical philosophy" (Berg 2021, 733). Kant himself called it a "paradox" that "respect for a mere idea" – namely the moral law – "is yet to serve as an inflexible precept of the will" (4:439).

Recently, there has been growing interest in Kant's conception of emotions and feelings in general,[2] and in Kant's conception of moral respect in particular.[3] This interest is motivated by the variety of roles that respect plays in Kant's philosophical work. It not only concerns moral motivation in the narrower sense but also the question of autonomy and freedom, of moral imputability, and of moral education. Kant made several "extremely cryptic" (Allison 1990, 125), "enigmatic," and "puzzling" (McCarty 1993, 421) statements about the "singular" (*sonderbar*) and "peculiar" (*eigentümlich*) (5:76) status of respect, attributing the following seven characteristics to it:[4]

---

[1] The Cambridge Translations of Kant's works mainly translate "Achtung" with "respect," whereas they translate "Ehrfurcht" with "reverence." However, Kant himself translates "Achtung" with the Latin word "reverentia" (6:402; 6:436).

[2] See, among others, Grenberg (2013), Cohen (2014), Cohen (2017), Guyer (2018), Merritt (2018), Sorensen/Williams (2018), Cohen (2020). Here and in what follows I will cite the literature chronologically.

[3] See, among others, DeWitt (2014), Ware (2014), Ware (2015), Guyer (2016), Cohen (2018, 17–21), Noller (2019), Berg (2021), Kriegel/Timmons (2021), Walschots (2022), Kolomý (2023), Walschots (2024).

[4] Broadie/Pybus (1975) distinguishes four characteristics, Reath (1989, 287) distinguishes two aspects, Allison (1990, 125) distinguishes "at least three aspects," Klemme (2007, 238), distinguishes between a formal, emotive and autonomous dimension, Singleton (2007, 42) distinguishes "four different contexts in which Kant discusses respect," Ameriks (2010, 30) lists "at least three features," Goy (2010, 157) distinguishes three "ethical functions," Wood (2010, 563) distinguishes "two related concepts of respect," and Berg (2021, 730) identifies "two elements."

(i) it has a purely rational origin,⁵ and it is therefore distinguished from empirical feelings⁶ (I shall refer to this as the Rationality Thesis);
(ii) it is considered as "the sole and also the undoubted moral incentive"⁷ (I shall refer to this point as the Singularity Thesis);
(iii) it is both negative and positive with regard to its emotional content⁸ (I shall refer to this as the Emotion Thesis);
(iv) in feeling respect, the human self is at the same time bound and free⁹ (I shall refer to this as the Freedom Thesis);
(v) it is "morality itself subjectively considered as an incentive"¹⁰ (I shall refer to this as the Subjectivity Thesis);
(vi) it primarily refers to a nonempirical object, an abstract "law," and not to individual human persons¹¹ (I shall refer to this as the Intentionality Thesis);
(vii) it is not a moral duty but the "basis" (*Grund*) for moral duties,¹² and we have the duty to cultivate it and show it to other persons¹³ (I shall refer to this as the Normativity Thesis).

---

⁵ "[T]hough respect is a feeling, it is not one received by means of influence; it is, instead, a feeling *self-wrought* by means of a rational concept" (4:401n.); "respect for the moral law is a feeling that is produced by an intellectual ground, and this feeling is the only one that we can cognize completely a priori and the necessity of which we can have insight into" (5:73); "[T]his feeling, on account of its origin, cannot be called pathologically effected but must be called practically effected" (5:75); "The feeling [scil. of respect] ... is not pathological, as would be a feeling produced by an object of the senses, but practical only, that is, possible through a preceding (objective) determination of the will and causality of reason" (5:80).
⁶ It is "specifically different from all feelings of the first kind, which can be reduced to inclination or fear" (4:401n). Respect is caused by the "influence of a mere intellectual idea on feeling" (5:80). Respect is a "special kind of feeling, which, however, does not precede the lawgiving of practical reason but is instead produced only by it" (5:92).
⁷ "Respect for the moral law is ... the sole and also the undoubted moral incentive" (5:78); Respect is "a singular feeling" and is of a "peculiar" (5:76) and "special kind" (6:402).
⁸ It "is regarded as an object neither of inclination nor of fear, though it has something analogous to both" (4:401n.); "on the one side [it] is merely *negative* but on the other side, and indeed with respect to the restricting ground of pure practical reason, it is *positive*" (5:74); "[I]t ... contains in it no pleasure but instead, so far, displeasure .... On the other hand ... it also contains something *elevating*" (5:80). "[T]he moral law unavoidably humiliates every human being when he compares with it the sensible propensity of his nature" (5:74); "however, since this constraint is exercised only by the lawgiving of his *own* reason, it also contains something *elevating*" (5:80).
⁹ "The consciousness of a free submission of the will to the law, yet as combined with an unavoidable constraint put on all inclinations though only by one's own reason, is respect for the law" (5:80).
¹⁰ "[R]espect for the law is not the incentive to morality; instead it is morality itself subjectively considered as an incentive" (5:76).
¹¹ "Any respect for a person is properly only respect for the law (of integrity and so forth) of which he gives us an example" (4:401n.).
¹² "It cannot be said that a man *has* a duty of respect toward himself, for he must have respect for the law within himself in order even to think of any duty whatsoever" (6:403).
¹³ "[R]espect ... is the basis (*Grund*) of certain duties" (6:403). A person "must have respect for the law within himself in order even to think of any duty whatsoever" (6:403); "Every man has

In this Element, I shall refer to these seven – seemingly contradictory – theses as the "puzzle of respect." Regarding the "curious combination of roles" (McBeath 1973, 283) that respect plays, Richard McCarty has argued that "some mystery still shrouds the peculiar feeling" (McCarty 1993, 434) and that it is characterized by interpretative "quandaries" (McCarty 1994, 15). Karl Ameriks has pointed out with regard to Kant's theses: "This can all sound too remarkable to be true" (Ameriks 2010, 31). Allen Wood (2010, 563) has called respect "a complex and even an ambivalent feeling." Furthermore, Melissa Zinkin (2006, 31) has stated that "Kant's discussion of the feeling of respect presents a puzzle regarding both the precise nature of this feeling and its role in his moral theory as an incentive that motivates us to follow the moral law."[14] Paul Guyer (2012, 421) argues that the role that respect plays in Kant's philosophy is "obscure." Due to its obscurity, Richard McCarty has restricted his analysis of respect only to "the role Kant supposes it plays in moral motivation" but has "not attempted any explanation of its etiology or phenomenology" (1993, 434).

Indeed, the status of Kant's conception of moral respect – as *reason's own feeling* – is "far from clear" (Ware 2014, 727). Jeanine Grenberg (2013, 49) speaks of "the mysterious idea that the moral law causes a feeling of respect" and a "distinctive feeling with an admittedly mysterious rational cause" (Grenberg 2011, 466), and argues for an integrative account of respect: "The future of Kantian ethics rests ... on the willingness of more commentators to welcome the fuller integration of feeling into the grounding of *a priori* morality which Kant's common grounding of morality encourages" (Grenberg 2011, 471). This calls for the consideration of the moral feeling of respect not only regarding Kant's moral philosophy but also his transcendental philosophy, anthropology, aesthetics, and pedagogy. To be sure, Kant himself was aware of his puzzling statements, conceding in a *Groundwork* footnote that "[i]t could be objected that I only seek refuge, behind the word respect, in an obscure feeling, instead of distinctly resolving the question by means of a concept of reason" (4:401 n.). It seems, however, that Kant did not fully resolve the question as originally intended.

In this Element, I will focus not only on the motivational role of respect, but also on its etiology, which requires consideration not only of Kant's moral psychology, but also his transcendental philosophy and his distinction between the noumenal and the sensible. McCarty has put this as follows: "Kant's interest in human action overlaps with his broader, metaphysical theories of freedom

---

a legitimate claim to respect from his fellow men and is *in turn* bound to respect every other" (6:463).

[14] For an overview of further critiques of Kant's theory of the moral feeling of respect, see Bagnoli (2003, 484) and Berg (2021, 734–5).

and causation, which are topics that today's action theorists generally wish to avoid" (McCarty 2009, xiii). Although Richard McCarty (1993, 434) has argued that "Kant himself placed respect's etiology beyond the limits of explanation," my interpretation is supported by Kant himself, who, in view to the moral feeling of respect, argues: "here we have the first and perhaps the only case in which we can determine a priori from concepts the relation of a cognition (here the cognition of a pure practical reason) to the feeling of pleasure or displeasure" (5:73).

In this Element, I shall attempt to make sense of Kant's seven aforementioned theses about respect and give a coherent and systematic account of it. In doing so, I assume that Kant develops a unified account of moral respect throughout his philosophical work. To this end, I will not only refer to Kant's ethics and moral psychology, but also his more general framework of transcendental idealism. I will argue that we can only understand Kant's conception of respect if we situate it within a larger conceptual framework that incorporates transcendental, practical, anthropological, pedagogical, and aesthetic dimensions. This calls for relating the moral feeling of respect to the three human faculties of the mind (5:198; 20:245) within Kant's philosophy, namely, to the understanding as the faculty of cognition, to the feeling of pleasure and displeasure as the power of judgment, and to the faculty of desire as (practical) reason.[15]

I will argue, however, that the overall framework, within which Kant's conception of respect must be interpreted to make sense of all its features, is his theory of moral autonomy[16] and will, which I shall distinguish from his conception of freedom as choice.[17] Drawing on Kant's complex notion of will and considering moral respect within the larger framework of his conception of autonomy allows me to connect it to the concepts of causality, self-consciousness, reason, and of sensibility, and to systematically locate it within Kant's transcendental philosophy. This systematic interpretation of Kant's conception of respect will also allow me to address the seven characteristics from various perspectives of his philosophical work on a broad textual basis. Thereby, I will not only focus on Kant's second *Critique* as many interpreters

---

[15] For a discussion of Kant's conception of rational feelings with regard to the faculties of the human mind, see Cohen (2018, 13). Walschots (2024, 7) has stressed the importance of Kant's "tri-partite theory of the faculties of the human mind" for understanding the moral feeling of respect.

[16] Henrich (1994, 108) has systematically linked respect to autonomy. However, he mainly focuses on the role of (pure) practical reason but not on the importance of the concept of will. Likewise, Allison (1990, 125) has argued that Kant's notion of respect is "intimately connected with his conception of autonomy."

[17] For a discussion of the problem of autonomy and choice in Kant and his early successors, see Noller (2024).

do,[18] but also his *Groundwork*, his *Religion*, his *Metaphysics of Morals*, as well as his first and third *Critique*.

To bring the puzzle of respect closer to a solution, this Element is structured as follows. In Section 2, I will discuss the question of what kind of entity respect is, and I will situate Kant's concept of respect regarding related concepts such as feeling, cognition, interest, incentive, will, and choice. I shall interpret the volitional structure of moral respect with regard to the autonomy of reason and argue that the autonomy of moral respect is not sufficient for imputable action but still demands freedom of choice, which Kant discusses in his *Religion* and in his *Metaphysics of Morals*. Furthermore, I situate the moral feeling of respect within Kant's system of the faculties of the mind. Section 3 discusses Kant's conception of moral respect with regard to related moral phenomena such as moral sense, compassion, and love. It first presents the concept of moral sense in the previous work of Shaftesbury and Hutcheson, and shows for what reasons Kant criticizes their theories. In doing so, the section addresses Kant's "Singularity Thesis." Section 4 is devoted to the questions of how moral respect is grounded in Kant's philosophy, and how respect grounds Kant's theory of moral motivation. After situating moral respect within Kant's ethics from a systematic point of view, two important approaches to understanding Kant's conception of respect are discussed, first described by McCarty (1993, 423), which he calls intellectualism and affectivism. Intellectualists conceive of respect as a purely rational attitude or judgment, whereas affectivists emphasize the role of respect as a (rational) feeling, without which a full account of respect must be incomplete. Drawing on Kant's complex notion of the will, I will argue for an alternative account to ground respect in Kant's works beyond intellectualism and affectivism, which I shall call the volitionalist account of respect (see Section 4.1). According to the volitionalist account, the key concept for understanding the seven aforementioned characteristics is neither reason nor sensibility but the autonomous will. Referring to Kant's complex notion of the autonomous will allows me to address features associated with both intellectualism (judgment and cognition; see 5:75–6) and affectivism (feeling; see 5:222; 8:283), and to develop a unified account.

The volitionalist account is motivated by the fact that Kant, in his second *Critique*, discusses moral respect with regard to volitional concepts such as "moral interest," "maxim," and "incentive" (5:79). He identifies moral respect with the self-reflection of autonomy, namely with "[t]he consciousness of a *free* submission of the will to the law, yet as combined with an unavoidable

---

[18] See for example Zinkin (2006), Metz (2004), Ware (2014), Ware (2015). Berg (2021) has emphasized the importance of Kant's third *Critique* for understanding moral respect.

constraint put on all inclinations though only by one's own reason" (5:80). In addition, Kant defines "respect as consciousness of direct necessitation of the will by the law" (5:117).

In his *Groundwork*, Kant deeply links moral respect to "an activity of a will." There, he argues that "[o]nly what is connected with my will merely as a ground and never as effect ... can be an object of respect" (4:400). According to the volitionalist account, when we feel respect, we experience a manifestation in feeling of an activity of the will, namely the autonomy of pure practical reason. Kant calls respect for the moral law a "maxim," namely that "of complying with such a law even if it infringes upon all my inclinations" (4:400–1). This shows that in moral respect, will, feeling and reason are closely connected. I will further explore this relationship in Section 5.3 with regard to the faculties of the mind involved in moral respect.

Referring to Kant's concept of the will allows me to argue for a compatibilist account of moral respect, according to which intellectualism and affectivism are true. This volitionalist reading allows me to interpret respect from a third-person perspective of pure practical reason and moral autonomy, and from a second-person perspective regarding the intentionality of respect (Section 5: Reason's Self-Consciousness), from a phenomenological first-person perspective of the individual agent (Section 7: Feeling Reason), and finally, from a second-person perspective of moral education (Section 8: Cultivating Morality). Section 5 discusses the transcendental framework of moral respect in terms of what Kant calls a "causality of reason" and a "causality of freedom." It thereby discusses respect from the perspective of Kant's transcendental philosophy and moral anthropology. It also focuses on Kant's distinction between the intelligible and the empirical character to reconstruct the transcendental framework of moral respect. I propose a compatibilist account of respect, which is distinct from both intellectualism and affectivism. I will demonstrate how respect is related to human nature, which is characterized by both rationality and sensibility. As such, moral respect is rooted in the human will, which does not necessarily align with the moral law a priori. In doing so, the section addresses not only the Rationality Thesis, but also the Subjectivity Thesis and the Intentionality Thesis. In Section 6, I discuss the impact of moral respect with regard to the problem of rational moral motivation. I show the special role that moral respect plays with regard to self-love and self-conceit. I distinguish between three models to understand the role of respect in moral motivation, and I reconstruct its negative effect upon human sensibility in terms of a moral judgment. Thereby, I address the Freedom Thesis and one part of the Emotion Thesis. The other part of the Emotion Thesis will be discussed in Section 7, which is devoted to the phenomenology of respect and its relationship to the feeling of the sublime. I will refer to Kant's *Critique of the Power of Judgment* and highlight the aesthetic role of moral respect and that of the faculty of (reflective) judgment. This lays the ground for Section 8, which is devoted to the Normativity Thesis. Therein, I discuss the question of how we can cultivate respect by means of moral education and how we can be responsible for acting from moral respect. I also discuss the question whether we have the duty to feel and show respect toward others, how respect, duty, and virtue are related, and how we fail to feel and show respect toward other persons. I discuss possible ways to combine respect with love, compassion and friendship, and how the cultivation of respect contributes to moral virtue and moral character. In the final Section 9, I address the seven characteristics of moral respect that constitute the "puzzle of respect" in context and attempt to solve it in light of the previous sections.

2 Situating Respect: Feeling, Cognition, Will, and Choice

2.1 Respect and Moral Psychology

Kant's concept of moral respect is situated between other moral psychological concepts such as incentive, motive, interest, and maxim, which only apply to finite rational beings such as humans. The same holds for the concept of moral respect. However, it is not clear at all what kind of entity respect actually is, given Kant's various and seemingly confusing characterizations.[19] Respect is sometimes understood as a moral feeling,[20] as a moral attitude,[21] representation or judgment,[22] or as a moral incentive (*Triebfeder*).[23] I shall call the first one the feeling approach,[24] the second one the judgment approach,[25] and the third one the motivation approach. All three interpretations have their own benefits and problems.

At a first glance, conceiving of respect as a feeling does justice to Kant's own terminology, because he explicitly calls respect a "feeling" in many places (e.g. 4:401 n.; 5:73; 5:75; 5:92). At the same time, respect, according to Kant, is not a heteronomous or "pathological" feeling, such as "inclination or fear" (4:401 n.) but a "special kind of feeling" (5:92), which, as an effect, is related to causes that Kant calls the "intellectual" (5:73), "rational" (4:401 n.) and

---

[19] From a systematic point of view, respect has been discussed as "a mode of behavior, a form of treatment, a kind of valuing, a type of attention, a motive, an attitude, a feeling, a tribute, a principle, a duty, an entitlement, a moral virtue, an epistemic virtue" (Dillon 2022).
[20] Metz (2004), Geiger (2011), Frierson (2014), Kriegel/Timmons (2021, 78), Kolomý (2023).
[21] Reath (1989, 287), Allison (1990, 123), Kriegel/Timmons (2021, 78), Walschots (2022).
[22] De Witt (2014, 39). [23] Herrera (2000), Lipscomb (2010, 61), Walschots (2024, 3).
[24] This approach is currently discussed as "affectivism."
[25] This approach is currently discussed as "intellectualism."

"practical" (5:75). Kant describes the complex causal structure of respect as being "*self-wrought*" (4:401 n.), "produced" (5:73) or "effected" by a rational "origin" (5:75). It must be "regarded as the *effect* of the law on the subject, and not as the *cause* of the law" (4:401 n.). I shall call this Kant's "Causality Thesis." According to Kant's Causality Thesis, respect is the effect of the moral law but at the same time, as the subjective determination of the will, a kind of cause, which Kant calls a "causality of freedom."

We need to further distinguish Kant's account of causation with regard to moral respect. Kant argues that the moral law causally determines the will objectively, whereas the moral feeling of respect determines the will subjectively as an "effect" of an intelligible cause (5:75). I propose to understand the effects of these causalities in terms of different kinds of determination, namely in terms of formal cause and efficient cause,[26] which I shall interpret in terms of normative and motivating reasons within Kant's system of the faculties of the mind.

Kant's Causality Thesis has led some interpreters – the so called "intellectualists" (McCarty 1993, 423) – to understand respect not as a feeling but rather as a rational attitude or judgment. This view is supported by some of Kant's statements, according to which respect is a purely rational mental activity such as the moral "consciousness of a free submission of the will to the law" (5:80) and "the representation of a worth that infringes upon my self-love" (4:401 n). Having said that, we must keep in mind that Kant does not identify the moral feeling of respect with rational activity as such, but rather describes it as being *caused* by the moral law (5:75). This leaves the question open whether the feeling of respect is a mere "*epiphenomenon*" (Sytsma 1993, 121) or whether it emerges from the moral law in such a way that it has a moral causal effect. Finally, respect can be understood not only as a feeling or as a rational attitude or judgment, but also as a volitional phenomenon, since Kant calls it "the sole and also the undoubted moral incentive" (5:78). However, this seems to be contradicted by the fact that Kant argues that "respect for the law is not the incentive to morality; instead it is morality itself subjectively considered as an incentive" (5:76).

2.2 Respect and Moral Motivation

In the chapter on the incentives of pure practical reason, Kant conceives of the concept of a determining ground in causal terms, given that he speaks of "effects" (5:72; 5:75) of the determining grounds of the moral law on the human will. The reason why I interpret the determining grounds in causal

---

[26] For this distinction, see Maimon (1791, 76–7).

terms is that this allows connecting it to Kant's conception of a "causality of reason," as well as connecting the problem of moral respect to the problem of transcendental freedom. The fact that Kant speaks of various kinds of causal relations of the moral law toward the moral feeling of respect, which I will interpret in terms of formal cause and efficient cause, allows us to discuss it with regard to the problem of internalism and externalism concerning moral motivation and of normative and motivating reasons.[27] Kant argues that the moral law is (i) the objective, (ii) the formal, (iii) the material, and (iv) the subjective determining ground of the will (4:400; 5:75). The moral law is the formal and objective cause in that it demands us to universalize our maxims and allows for the cognition of practical objects. Kant says that the morally goodwill is determined by the pure form of the moral law, and that this form of the law is objective (5:28–29; 5:31). However, the moral law is at the same time the subjective determining ground of the morally goodwill in terms of an efficient cause insofar as it effects the moral feeling of respect, considered as a moral interest from a volitional point of view.

The debate about moral motivation often refers to the concept of a judgment. Kant himself discusses moral respect in many places in his second *Critique* in terms of a "judgment of reason" (5:75; 5:76; 5:78), thereby referring to the philosophical tradition of free choice in terms of *arbitrium liberum* (6:213). Concerning the relationship between moral judgment and moral motivation, two questions arise: First, "do moral judgments motivate *necessarily* or do they motivate only *contingently*? Second, can moral judgments motivate on their own or can they motivate only by the intermediation of a desire or other conative state?" (Rosati 2016). Whereas internalism about moral motivation claims "that a necessary connection exists between sincere moral judgment and either justifying reasons or motives," externalism claims that "any connection that exists between moral judgment and motivation is purely contingent" (Rosati 2016).

To be sure, Kant denies that the moral feeling of respect grounds morality by justifying it, as the moral sense in Shaftesbury and Hutcheson does. It "does not precede the lawgiving of practical reason" (5:92), and "[i]t does not serve for appraising actions and certainly not for grounding the objective moral law itself" (5:76). However, according to his Subjectivity Thesis, Kant considers moral respect as "morality itself subjectively considered as an incentive" (5:76). This allows understanding moral respect both in terms of normative and motivating reasons. Normative reasons play both a deontic and a deliberative

---

[27] Schadow (2013, 67) discusses the moral feeling of respect with regard to internalism and externalism in terms of moral reasons, however not with regard to moral imputability.

role, and "the deliberative role of normative reasons makes them potential motivating reasons" (Alvarez/Way 2024).

From the perspective of the autonomy of reason, moral respect seems to be a kind of moral internalism, as Kant speaks of "respect as consciousness of direct necessitation of the will by the law" (5:117). The normativity of the moral law is causally directly, that is, *internally*, related to the determination of the will, because the moral law is its objective and formal determining ground. Furthermore, as the subjective determining ground of the will, the moral law "produces" (5:73) the moral feeling of respect in terms of a motivating reason, although it is merely "conducive to the influence of the law upon the will" (5:75) as Kant says shortly after. Here the question arises of whether this "direct necessitation of the will" is sufficient for moral action or whether it demands election by the faculty of choice as well.[28]

As I shall argue later, we need to understand the moral law's direct necessitation not in terms of motivating reasons but in terms of normative reasons. As such, Kant holds neither an internalism nor an externalism about moral motivation but a kind of hybrid internalism. According to this interpretation, Kant's thesis that respect is "morality itself subjectively *considered* as an incentive" (5:76; emphasis mine) need not be understood in terms of immediate motivation or necessitation to an action but in terms of *reflection*, which implies choice.

2.3 Respect and Moral Choice

With regard to the question of whether and how moral respect leads to a moral action, there are two opposing camps in research, which I shall call determinists and electivists. Determinists argue that the moral law is, by means of respect, both necessary and sufficient to bring about a moral action.[29] Electivists, however, argue that moral respect is only necessary but not sufficient for moral action. Whereas the moral feeling of respect determines the will, it does not determine our faculty of choice.[30] I will explain this distinction in more detail later with regard to respect. According to weak electivism, respect

---

[28] This problem of Kant's internalism about moral motivation has been discussed in research. McCarty (1993, 427) criticizes internalism from the perspective of human frailty. Similarly, Herrera (2000, 397) argues that "intellectualist interpretations are incorrect, because they take the moral *Beweggrund* to determine the will directly, without mediation." Klemme (2006, 137) argues with regard to the moral feeling of respect that moral reasons motivate us without determining our will. McCarty (2009, 174) argues that "we must suppose that the degree or quality of the moral law's determination of each individual's will is in some way up to the individual" (174). Walschots (2024, 21) argues that moral respect "ground[s] desire with impelling rather than efficient causation."

[29] See Henrich (1994, 93); Metz (2004); Guyer (2012, 422), Guyer (2016, 240), Berg (2021, 733).

[30] See Reath (1989, 297–8); Allison (1990, 26); McCarty (1994, 15), who speaks of Kant's "elective model," Klemme (2006, 137), Walschots (2024, 21).

for the moral law needs to be accompanied by choice to come to an action. According to strong electivism, we are even responsible for whether and how the moral law determines our will by the moral feeling of respect, from which follows that we have the duty to cultivate it. I shall call this kind of strong electivism "cultivism" about moral respect.

We find textual evidence for determinism and electivism in Kant's moral philosophy. In the chapter on the incentives of pure practical reason in his second *Critique* in particular, Kant uses metaphors of conflict that suggest that pure practical reason is realized in an action after having defeated the influences of inclination from the will.[31] In many places in this chapter, Kant speaks of pure practical reason and the moral law in terms of an acting subject. This suggests that it is not we who act by our faculty of choice, but a rational faculty within us. Kant says that the moral feeling of respect promotes the causality to act morally (5:75). He argues that the moral law "effects a feeling conducive to the influence of the law upon the will" (5:75). To be sure, promoting causality and being "conducive" (*beförderlich*) can be understood in a strong determinist and in a weak electivist sense. Likewise, Kant says that respect "supplies authority to the law," which does not imply that it necessarily leads to a moral action, and that it serves "as an incentive to make this law its maxim" (5:76). This seems to imply that it is not the moral law or the moral feeling of respect that "acts" in us but that we need to "make" it a maxim, that is to incorporate it into our maxim by choice.

An argument in favor of determinism about moral respect, however, is the fact that this interpretation takes seriously what Kant calls the autonomy of pure practical reason (5:43). According to Kant's conception of autonomy, pure practical reason must not only determine the will objectively and formally but also subjectively, such that it leads to a moral action. Hence, from the perspective of the autonomy of pure reason, there seems to be no room for electivism about moral respect, since a lack of respect would result in heteronomy insofar as the will is determined by external objects (4:441).

There are, indeed, more arguments that speak for electivism. If moral respect motivates us to moral action without choice, then we cannot explain how we should be *responsible* for the action. Respect, according to electivism, is only a necessary but not a sufficient condition of imputable moral action, as Kant argues in his *Religion* (6:27).[32] For otherwise, the determination of moral respect would lead to what the early post-Kantian debate on freedom of the

---

[31] For a critique of the metaphors of conflict of forces, see Reath (1989, 298n.), Allison (1990, 126), Herrera (2000, 397), and Ware (2014, 743).
[32] I would like to thank the anonymous reviewer for drawing my attention to this problem.

will has called an "intelligible fatalism" (Schmid 1790).[33] With regard to the rationalist pre-Kantian tradition, Walschots (2024, 10) has argued that we need to understand Kant's notion of an incentive (*Triebfeder*) according to Baumgarten's (and also Leibniz's) terminology in terms of an "impelling cause" that does not necessitate our action but only "encourages" it. To maintain moral responsibility, respect must only facilitate the moral determination of will to an action but not be sufficient for individual choice, as I will argue in Section 8.[34]

Electivism about moral respect is supported by many of Kant's statements. In his *Religion*, he argues that "the free power of choice incorporates moral feeling into its maxim" so that "[t]he subjective ground ... of our incorporating this incentive into our maxims seems to be an addition to personality" (6:27–8). Thereby, the "predisposition to personality is the susceptibility to respect for the moral law *as of itself a sufficient incentive to the power of choice*." However, according to Kant's distinction between will and choice, "this is possible only because the free power of choice incorporates moral feeling into its maxim" (6:27). As I will show later, Kant's "Incorporation Thesis" (Allison 1990, 40) is particularly relevant to the question of what role respect plays in terms of freedom of choice and autonomy.

Likewise, Kant in his *Metaphysics of Morals* distinguishes between will and choice. He claims that "[l]aws proceed from the will, *maxims* from choice. In man the latter is a capacity for free choice; the will, which is directed to nothing beyond the law itself, cannot be called either free or unfree, since it is not directed to actions but immediately to giving laws for the maxims of actions (and is, therefore, practical reason itself)" (6:226). From this quotation follows that freedom of choice is realized if we incorporate the incentive of moral respect into our maxim. Therefore, the moral feeling of respect is not directly causing our moral action, as a determinist reading suggest; "[w]e have, rather, a *susceptibility* on the part of free choice to be moved by pure practical reason (and its law), and this is what we call moral feeling" (6:400). Considered from the perspective of freedom of choice, respect "is to be understood as the *maxim* of limiting our self-esteem by the dignity of humanity in another person" (6:449).

However, Timmermann (2022, 103) has called Allison's electivism an intellectualism, referring to his thesis that the spontaneity of election is "the capacity

---

[33] For a textual translation and discussion of the early post-Kantian debate on the problem of intelligible fatalism, see Noller/Walsh (2022).
[34] From the perspective of moral imputability, Walschots (2024, 21) distinguishes between feeling and cognition in Kant's account of respect in order "to escape the intellectual determinism of Baumgarten's view."

to determine oneself to act on the basis of objective (intersubjectively valid) rational norms and, in light of these norms, to take (or reject) inclinations or desires as sufficient reasons for action" (Allison 1990, 5). Timmermann (2022, 103) criticizes that due to intellectualism, Allison's incorporation thesis is "committed to the thesis that, at the time of a wrongful act, we are deluded about our obligations." Let us assume that we fail to act out of respect for the moral law but instead due to self-conceit. How can this moral failure in our choice be explained? Opposed to Allison's intellectualism, Timmermann argues that Kant endorses a "hybrid theory of practical failure," thereby endorsing "intellectualism about non-moral action while defending a strongly anti-intellectualist or volitional position in the realm of moral choice." According to the hybrid model, "[m]oral failure is not caused by some cognitive defect or a flawed piece of reasoning. It consists in the conscious, knowing, voluntary choice not to will the moral end" (Timmermann 2022, 7). However, as I shall argue later, this hybrid account of immoral action underestimates the role of imputable self-deception in Kant's moral philosophy, where Kant's concept of rationalizing plays a major role.[35]

In what follows, I shall argue for a middle way between Allison's intellectual electivism and Timmermann's hybrid account of moral failure. I shall reject determinism about moral respect and argue for a conception of volitional electivism, according to which we are responsible for acting both from respect for the moral law and from self-conceit.[36] This will finally allow me to discuss respect in terms of moral education and cultivation, which Kant considers a duty, and discuss self-conceit in terms of imputable rationalizing and moral self-deception.

2.4 Respect and the Faculties of the Mind

In research, Kant's notion of respect has often been interpreted in terms of either a feeling (4:401 n.), a judgment (5:75), or an incentive (5:76). However, given the fact that feelings, judgments and incentives belong to different faculties of the mind, there are good reasons why respect should not be reduced to just one of three candidates – judgment, feeling or incentive – but rather be understood as a complex phenomenon that features these three aspects. This view is supported by the fact that Kant argues that "all faculties or capacities of the soul can be reduced to the three that cannot be further derived from a common ground: the faculty of cognition, the feeling of pleasure and displeasure, and the

---

[35] For the problem of imputable self-deception, see Ware (2014, 737), Noller (2021), Noller (2022).
[36] I am not discussing the case of acting permissibly in the pursuit of self-interest because it is not relevant in this context.

faculty of desire" (5:178).[37] A suitable conceptual candidate for unifying these three aspects of moral respect – judgment, feeling, and incentive – is the concept of *emotion*, a term which Kant himself admittedly does not use in his philosophy.[38] As Scarantino and de Sousa (2021) have argued, the concept of emotion entails both a descriptive dimension, concerning the "question of what the emotions are," and a normative dimension, concerning the "question of whether emotions are rational." The normative question is of special importance regarding the moral function of respect in Kant's ethics and intellectualist interpretations. In line with the previous interpretation of respect as (i) a feeling, (ii) a judgment, and (iii) an incentive, Scarantino and de Sousa (2021) argue "that emotions have historically been conceptualized in one of three main ways: as experiences, as evaluations, and as motivations." They criticize that "[e]motions have long been thought to score poorly in terms of both cognitive and strategic rationality." In contrast to this view and in line with Kant, they argue that "emotions have *cognitive bases*, which consist of cognitions whose function is to provide emotions with their particular objects." With regard to Kant's conception of the moral feeling of respect, I shall understand pure practical reason and the moral law as its "cognitive basis," which also explains respect's intentionality toward the moral law, which I shall discuss in Section 5.1. Understanding respect as an emotion will allow me to unify its various aspects within one single but complex concept, and to further analyze its rational basis, its intentionality, its normativity, and its phenomenology.

When considering the moral feeling of respect as a complex phenomenon within Kant's philosophy, it might be helpful to refer to Kant's third *Critique* to situate moral respect systematically within Kant's three *Critiques*. Whereas in his first *Critique*, Kant is especially interested the possibility of what he calls a "causality of freedom" and a "causality of reason," in his second *Critique* he applies the causality of freedom to the human will and its objects. Kant says, "it is still pure reason whose *cognition* here lies at the basis of its practical use" (5:16). Accordingly, by narrowing the focus, "sensibility is not regarded as a capacity for intuition at all but only as feeling (which can be a subjective ground of desire)" (5:90). Finally, in his third *Critique*, Kant discusses moral respect from the perspective of judgment and feeling, and from the perspective of the "system of all the faculties of the human mind" (20:205). He claims that

---

[37] For Kant's tri-partite theory of the faculties of the human mind, see Walschots (2024), 14. Walschots argues that "Kant assigns the role of an incentive to feeling and not cognition" (18). In what follows, I shall argue that an incentive is a volitional phenomenon that can be interpreted in terms of feeling and cognition.

[38] Kant uses the concepts of "feeling" (*Gefühl*), "affect" (*Affekt*), and "passions" (*Leidenschaften*).

> it is surely enough to produce a connection *a priori* between the feeling of pleasure and the other two faculties if we connect a cognition *a priori*, namely the rational concept of freedom, with the faculty of desire as its determining ground, at the same time subjectively finding in this objective determination a feeling of pleasure contained in the determination of the will. (20:206–7)

Considering the causal relationship between the moral law and the feeling of respect, Kant stresses that "in this way the faculty of cognition is not combined with the faculty of desire by means of the pleasure or displeasure, for this does not precede the latter faculty, but either first succeeds the determination of it, or else *is perhaps nothing other than the sensation of the determinability of the will through reason itself*, thus not a special feeling and distinctive receptivity that requires a special section under the properties of the mind" (20:207; my emphasis). This quotation shows that a volitionalist account of moral respect allows connecting it both with the faculty of understanding and the faculty of judgment. Since the moral feeling of respect is constituted a priori by the interaction of all three faculties of the mind, these faculties allow for a unity of the multi-faced phenomenon of moral respect.

3 Distinguishing Respect: Beyond Moral Sense, Compassion, and Love

Kant claims that respect is a "special kind of feeling" (5:92) and "the sole and also the undoubted moral incentive" (5:78). This claim requires a further demarcation from related feelings and concepts such as the moral sense, love, and compassion. In doing so, we can determine certain qualities that distinguish respect from other feelings according to Kant's Singularity Thesis, which describes respect as "specifically different from all feelings of the first kind, which can be reduced to inclination or fear" (4:401 n.). Even though the moral feeling of respect is distinguished from other feelings due to its origin, it is indistinguishable from them from a motivational point of view. Respect, as Kant puts it, "has exactly the same inward effect, that of an impulse to activity, as a feeling of the agreeableness expected from the desired action would have produced" (5:116). From a historical point of view, Kant explicitly distinguishes the moral feeling of respect from conceptions of the moral sense as developed before by Shaftesbury and Hutcheson.[39] These distinctions help us to better understand the historical formation of Kant's conception of moral motivation, to better understand the relationship between respect and the moral law, and to tackle both the Singularity Thesis and the Rationality Thesis about moral respect.

---

[39] For a discussion of Kant's relationship to Hutcheson and Shaftesbury, see Henrich (2009), Goy (2010), Walschots (2017), and Kolomý (2023).

3.1 Kant's Critique of Moral Sense

In his *Characteristics of Men, Manners, Opinions, Times* (1711), Shaftesbury had introduced a "sense of right and wrong," which he described as "being as natural to us as natural affection itself, and being a first principle in our constitution and make," so that "there is no speculative opinion, persuasion or belief which is capable immediately or directly to exclude or destroy it" (Shaftesbury 2000, 179). Similarly, Hutcheson in his *Inquiry into the Original of Our Ideas of Beauty and Virtue* (1725) had introduced the "moral sense," which he conceived as an epistemic faculty "by which we perceive Virtue and Vice, and approve or disapprove them in others" (Hutcheson 2004, 89). What is special about the moral sense is that it is independent from the faculty of desire. Hutcheson characterizes the moral sense in terms of "a Determination of the Mind, to receive any Idea from the Presence of an Object which occurs to us, independent on our Will" (Hutcheson 2004, 90). He argues that the moral sense is epistemically autonomous and cannot be changed by rational and volitional influences, like our perception of auditory or visual phenomena. The moral sense, as Hutcheson puts it, is an immediate faculty of perception of the moral beauty of an action. It is therefore independent from "any innate Ideas, Knowledge, or practical Proposition," and "antecedent to all Reason from Interest" so that it is "only a Determination of our Minds to receive amiable or disagreeable Ideas of Actions, when they occur to our Observation, antecedent to any Opinions of Advantage or Loss to redound to our selves from them" (Hutcheson 2004, 100; 112). The moral sense is, therefore, both pre-rational and pre-volitional, which means that its immediate and pure moral perception cannot be distorted by rational or volitional influences. As I shall argue later, Kant criticizes the concept of moral sense specifically because of its narrowly focused autonomy and independence from the faculty of (practical) reason and will. In addition, Kant argues that moral respect, in contrast to the moral sense, must not be antecedent to reason but rather its causal effect. Against the narrow focus of moral sense, Kant attempts to connect the concept of moral respect with the capacity of both reason and will, thereby giving practical reason the causal priority, which allows him to justify this feeling from a normative point of view and make it subject to moral imputability, education, and cultivation, as I shall argue in Section 8.

Kant mainly criticizes the conception of a moral sense for two reasons, which we can call the "contingency objection" and the "sensibility objection." From a historical point of view, Kant claims that the conception of moral sense is in line with "Epicurus, who reduced its [moral philosophy's] criteria to the sense of pleasure or pain" (2:396). Kant argues that the moral sense is "a contradiction"

(15:353) and only a "supposed special sense," because "feeling" is opposed to "what has to do merely with universal law," and because feelings are such that they "by nature differ infinitely from one another in degree," and cannot "furnish a uniform standard of good and evil, and one cannot judge validly for others by means of one's feeling" (4:442). Therefore, Hutcheson's conception of a moral sense and its "principle of sympathy" is only an instance of the principle of happiness, which basically only expresses our "empirical interest" (4:442 n.). According to Kant's contingency objection, the moral sense is not able to objectively justify our moral judgments but merely expresses an individual state that is not grounded by objective principles, since it is antecedent to reason. From Kant's metaethical point of view, the moral sense is therefore a non-cognitivist emotivist account.

We can summarize Kant's objections against the conception of moral sense as a kind of reductio ad absurdum (see 27:1325):

(1) The moral sense cannot be shown a priori but only from experience. [Sensibility Objection]
(2) What experience teaches us is accidental and does not provide any moral necessity. [Contingency Objection]
(3) The value of the moral action is therefore only in him who has a moral feeling.
(4) The value of moral action needs to be universal and independent of its being felt.
(5) If there is such a moral feeling in us, it must not precede the knowledge of the moral rule and make it possible, but only follow it.
(6) The moral sense precedes reason.
(7) The moral sense is no source of objective moral motivation.

3.2 Kant's Discussion of Moral Feelings

From Kant's general critique of the moral sense follows his discussion of moral feelings such as compassion and love, considered as the *primary* moral attitudes in particular. Kant speaks of "blind compassion" and argues that this feeling "disrupts justice" (20:29). The reason why Kant criticizes compassion and love as primary moral attitudes is that they lack a moral principle,[40] which is why Kant's contingency objection and sensibility objection also apply here:

> The sympathetic in man always stems from appearance, and not from the value of the thing; thus we find that compassion is mostly passion. It is a call

---
[40] In his *Metaphysics of Morals*, however, Kant discusses the relationship between love, compassion, and respect at greater length. I discuss this relationship in Section 8.

of nature which invites us to consider our duty here; but it is nothing more plaintive than a judge who dispenses justice according to compassion; for every one runs the risk of losing his case as soon as he has to do with persons who can whine well. (Anthropology Starke, 323)

Like compassion, Kant criticizes the inclination of love. Since love is a desire and follows the law of nature, it "cannot be commanded" (4:399). In other words, love is not subject to normativity, because it lacks rationality and is not directly causally related to the capacity of reason. We can only be commanded what we are in principle responsible for, since, according to Kant, "ought" implies "can" (6:45; 6:50). From a phenomenological perspective, compassion and love are feelings that are contingent, so that in feeling them, we are not able to form objective judgments. What distinguishes moral respect from compassion and love is the fact that the object of respect is not a special state of another person, but a set of rational and moral features one *shares* with the person one respects. In his *Groundwork*, Kant argues that "[a]ny respect for a person is properly only respect for the law (of integrity and so forth) of which he gives us an example" (4:401 n.). According to Kant's intentionality thesis, the object of respect exemplifies the moral law, insofar as it is *subject* to the moral law. Its ground is not feeling, which is arbitrary, but reason, which is objective and therefore allows constituting moral principles and justifying the moral feeling toward another person.

Kant describes the normative framework of a moral feeling that avoids the subjectivity and sensibility objection as being in a state of autonomy. As such, "[w]e stand under a *discipline* of reason" and "the authority of the law (although our own reason gives it)" (5:82). Prior to his late *Metaphysics of Morals*, Kant in his second *Critique* criticizes the moral attitudes of compassion and love, because they are not causally related to the moral law to allow for moral objectivity and justification. In the following quotation, Kant gives four reasons:

> Inclination is [i] *blind and servile*, whether it is kindly or not; and when morality is in question, reason must not play the part of mere guardian to inclination but, disregarding it altogether, must attend solely to its own interest as pure practical reason. Even this feeling of compassion and tender sympathy, if [ii] it *precedes consideration of what is duty* and [iii] *becomes the determining ground*, is itself burdensome to right-thinking persons, [iv] *brings their considered maxims into confusion*, and produces the wish to be freed from them and subject to lawgiving reason alone. (5:118; annotation and emphasis mine)

In this quote, Kant criticizes that feelings such as compassion and sympathy do not *as such* accord with the moral law insofar as they have their own principles of intentionality. Compassion is not directed to the general concept of duty but to the individual degree of pain that one sympathizes with. Depending on individual and empirical circumstances, however, does not allow providing an objective account of moral motivation. Compassion and sympathy are, according to Kant, unable to justify moral action and to correspond to moral normativity. However, Kant's preference for moral respect can be combined with compassion and love, as I will show in Section 8, where I discuss their relationship in more detail with regard to Kant's *Metaphysics of Morals*. This, however, requires that the moral feeling of respect is causally related to the moral law in the right way. As I shall argue in Section 5, respect is distinguished from similar phenomena such as love and compassion insofar as it is not directed toward individual persons but to a general normative structure which Kant calls "humanity." Kant calls this form the "the idea of humanity in our subject" (5:257) and "respect for the dignity of humanity in our own person" (5:273). I shall interpret this being directed to a supra-individual object as a special kind of normative relationship, which Kant calls the moral law. However, the fact that the moral feeling of respect is normatively distinguished from other feelings does not mean that it cannot be combined with them. In Section 8.3, I will show how respect can enter into moral relationships with love and compassion.

4 Grounding Respect: Beyond Affectivism and Intellectualism

The notion of moral respect is essential not only for Kant's theory of moral motivation but for his entire foundation of ethics, which is based on Kant's concept of pure practical reason. From a systematic point of view, moral respect has two functions: (i) *objectively* to serve as a causality of freedom, thereby realizing the autonomy of pure practical reason (Causality Condition), and (ii) *subjectively* to allow for actions for the sake of the moral law and not just conformably with it (Morality Condition). Together, both functions enable the autonomy of will. Kant connects both functions right at the beginning of chapter 3, "On the Incentives of Pure Practical Reason," of his second *Critique*, where he introduces the Morality Condition of respect:

> If the determination of the will takes place *conformably* with the moral law but only by means of a feeling, of whatever kind, that has to be presupposed in order for the law to become a sufficient determining ground of the will, so that the action is not done for the sake of the law, then the action will contain *legality* indeed but not *morality*. (5:71)

Whereas Kant had characterized the most important features of moral respect in the *Groundwork* footnote (4:401 n.), he discusses the systematic significance of respect for his ethics in the third chapter of his second *Critique*. Henry Allison (1990, 121) has emphasized the systematic importance of this chapter, as "the whole question of the adequacy of Kant's attempt to ground morality is reserved for the third part." However, the systematic position and grounding function of moral respect within Kant's ethics has rarely been discussed.[41] In this section, I shall discuss the causal relationship between the intelligible and feeling in terms of rational and normative grounding. By doing so, I shall address Kant's Rationality Thesis, according to which moral respect is "a feeling *self-wrought* by means of a rational concept" (4:401 n.), which is "produced by an intellectual ground" (5:73) and which is "possible through a preceding (objective) determination of the will and causality of reason" (5:80). I shall do so by referring to Kant's Causality Condition and his Morality Condition.

4.1 Volitionalism about Respect

Kant's Rationality Thesis, especially his reference to a "causality of reason," suggests discussing the grounding of moral respect not only from the systematic perspective of his moral philosophy but rather from transcendental philosophy in general. Therefore, I shall argue that to understand Kant's Rationality Thesis, we need to understand moral respect from the perspective of the human will that can be determined by pure practical reason. Kant argues that moral respect is not caused by the influence of sensibility upon the human will but by pure practical reason, understood as a causality of freedom. The moral law is, as Kant claims, "subjectively a ground of respect" (5:74). This allows him to understand moral respect in terms of autonomy and morality, and to distinguish it from alternative moral feelings such as love and compassion that are causally related to and grounded in sensibility. At the same time, Kant stresses that the moral feeling of respect is not to be confused with an "intellectual feeling" (5:117), as he puts it.[42] According to Kant, we must avoid the "illusion" to understand the "subjective side of this intellectual determinability of the will as something aesthetic and the effect of a special sensible feeling" (5:117). The moral feeling of respect as such is not a subjective determining ground of the human will. Rather, it is a causal effect of the moral law that is mediated by the faculty of desire. The volitionalist account of respect draws on this mediating role of the faculty of desire.

---

[41] For a systematic discussion of the moral feeling of respect, see Lauener (1981), Henrich (1994), Metz (2004), Schadow (2013), Noller (2016), Noller (2019), and Timmermann (2022, 32–3).

[42] In his third *Critique*, however, Kant calls the moral feeling of respect a *"spiritual* feeling" (5:335). This apparent contradiction can be resolved if we understand Kant's denial of an intellectual feeling in terms of his transcendental critique of an intellectual intuition (B 72). Whereas an intellectual feeling would be produced by intellectual intuition, a spiritual one is produced by pure practical reason.

Kant's "first question" in his second *Critique* is "whether pure reason of itself alone suffices to determine the will or whether it can be a determining ground of the will only as empirically conditioned" (5:15). Kant links this basic moral question to the basic transcendental question of a causality of freedom that he had discussed in the first *Critique* before. There, Kant had argued that "[e]verything is practical that is possible through freedom" (B 828). In his second *Critique*, Kant clarifies that "[b]y a concept of an object of practical reason I understand the representation of an object as an effect possible through freedom" (5:57). This shows that the systematic framework of moral respect extends beyond the practical realm to the theoretical and transcendental.

From a practical point of view, the concept of a causality of reason can be applied to the human will that is determined by the moral law. Kant thereby discusses moral respect in terms of a practical cognition. In opposition to theoretical cognition, practical cognition "is not concerned with cognition of the constitution of objects that may be given to reason from elsewhere but rather with a cognition insofar as it can itself become the ground of the existence of objects and insofar as reason, by this cognition, has causality in a rational being, that is, pure reason, which can be regarded as a faculty immediately determining the will" (5:46). In contrast to theoretical cognition, practical cognition has "to do only with determining grounds of the will" (5:20). With regard to practical reason, Kant argues that "now we have to do with a will and have to consider reason not in its relation to objects but in relation to this will and its causality" (5:16) Thus, we can see that Kant shifts the perspective in his second *Critique* from the transcendental causality of reason as such to the human will. Accordingly, from the systematic perspective of practical reason, "sensibility is not regarded as a capacity for intuition at all but only as feeling (which can be a subjective ground of desire)" (5:90). Here we see that Kant directly links the concept of a feeling to the concept of the will. This allows us to understand moral respect from a volitionalist point of view, which covers crucial features of affectivism. What is important about this characterization of practical cognition is that Kant describes these volitional states in his third *Critique* in terms of *feeling*: "The state of mind of a will determined by something . . . is in itself already a feeling of pleasure and is identical with it" (5:222).[43] Likewise, Kant argues in his *Theory and Practice* essay that "the will's receptivity to finding itself subject to the law as unconditional necessitation is called *moral feeling*, which is therefore not the cause but the effect of the determination of the will" (8:283).[44]

---

[43] Berg (2021, 740) has emphasized the role of this quotation for understanding moral respect, however not with regard to a volitionalist reading of respect, which I have developed in Noller (2019).

[44] Baxley (2010, 149) has pointed to this passage; however, she does not discuss the moral feeling of respect from a volitionalist perspective.

Practical cognition needs intuition much like theoretical cognition does, however without thereby being dependent on *external* sense data, as theoretical cognition does. Instead, Kant is referring to the structure of the will, which serves as a kind of a priori intuition, which is compatible with a priori feeling without being an *intellectual* intuition, which is impossible according to Kant's first *Critique*. Like in the case of theoretical cognition, where it is "necessary to make the mind's concepts sensible" (B 75), for practical cognition we need to make the moral law sensible in terms of moral respect, albeit without being dependent on heteronomous sensibility and inclinations. In cognizing theoretical objects, we are "given" objects and are "affected" by sensibility. The objects of practical reason, however, are not constituted like objects of theoretical cognition as a unity of internal concepts and external intuition (B 75). Rather, they are internally and volitionally brought about "as an effect possible through freedom" (5:57), which explains Kant's Causality Thesis, according to which the moral feeling of respect is "*self-wrought* by means of a rational concept" (4:401 n.) Kant says that "[t]he only objects of a practical reason are ... those of the *good* and the *evil*" (5:58), and since we bring them about through freedom, we are ultimately responsible for them.

4.2 Intellectualism and Affectivism

Considering the problematic conceptual status of respect between reason and feeling in Kant's ethics, which concerns both the Rationality Thesis and the Emotion Thesis, Richard McCarty (1993, 423) has famously coined the terms "intellectualist" and "affectivist":

> Intellectualists hold that respect for the moral law is, or arises from, a purely intellectual recognition of the supreme authority of the moral law, *and* that this intellectual recognition is sufficient to generate moral action independently of any special motivating feelings or affections. Opposed to the intellectualist interpretation is what I shall call the *affectivist* view. Affectivists need not deny that Kantian moral motivation initially arises from an intellectual recognition of the moral law. Contrary to intellectualists, however, they maintain that it also depends on a peculiar moral feeling of respect for law.

In research, there is a variety of forms of intellectualism and affectivism about moral respect.[45] From an intellectualist point of view, Sytsma (1993, 121) has argued that the moral feeling of respect "is the result of the already motivating power of reason" and therefore a mere "*epiphenomenon* of moral motivation." This means that the moral feeling of respect only accompanies the causality of

---

[45] For an overview and critique of intellectualism, see Herrera (2000, 397–400), Berg (2021, 735n.), and Walschots (2024, 2n.); for affectivism, see Ware (2014, 741n.) and Berg (2021, 737n.).

pure practical reason but does not have in itself a causal or systematic role. Allison (1990, 123) has argued that respect "consists simply in the recognition of its supremely authoritative character." Guyer (2016, 240) proposes a kind of hybrid intellectualism by distinguishing between the noumenal and the phenomenal, arguing that even if "the feeling of respect is ultimately an epiphenomenon of the noumenal determination of the will, the feeling of respect could still be supposed to play an indispensable causal role in the phenomenal process that expresses the noumenal determination of the will to abide by the moral law." According to my volitional account of respect, however, the noumenal and the phenomenal can be understood as two aspects of the same will.

Affectivists such as McCarty (1993, 442–3) argue for "the necessary role of moral feeling in Kantian moral motivation," which is "consequent to the initial recognition or moral judgment the intellectualists emphasize exclusively." Against intellectualism, which only considers the Causality Condition, I shall argue that we need to take into account the subjective emotional role of respect to do justice to the Morality Condition, that is, to extend legality to morality. In other words: the Morality Condition demands that there is moral subjectivity involved in moral motivation, which can be further explained in terms of moral feeling and volitional self-consciousness. At the same time, affectivism cannot explain the unity of rationality and feeling, as Kant expresses it in his Rationality Thesis. Ware (2014, 734) has criticized affectivism insofar as it "only considers respect as a feeling with varying strength, but the notion of 'strength' does not speak to the experience of moral feeling from the agent's own point of view" and argued for "a suitably idealized phenomenology, rather than a model of competing forces." Similarly, Berg (2021, 737) has argued that "affectivists meet trouble ... when they try to explain precisely how respect differs from ordinary feelings in a way that could legitimize its involvement in moral motivation." To be sure, affectivism is compatible with the intellectual aspect of respect, because McCarty (1993, 423) argues that affectivism "need not deny that Kantian moral motivation initially arises from an intellectual recognition." However, following the criticism by Ware (2014) and Berg (2021), I will argue that only the volitionalist interpretation allows us to understand respect as a *moral* feeling, because the faculty of will allows us to *connect* the faculty of feeling with the faculty of reason, and to understand and evaluate feelings from a normative point of view. As such, the volitionalist interpretation allows us to understand how moral feelings can be cultivated, and how we can be held responsible for cultivating moral feelings, because it recognizes the faculty of will as mediating between reason and sensibility.

Considering the two seemingly irreconcilable positions of intellectualism and affectivism, there have been various attempts to overcome both approaches.

Frierson (2014, 150) has argued that "intellectualists are correct about the claims that the moral law must motivate directly, and not by means of a feeling. ... But affectionists are correct that the moral law motivates by means of a moral feeling." He argues that we can reconcile both seemingly contradictory positions in terms of Kant's antinomies, namely by referring to the transcendental distinction between things-in-themselves and appearances. In a similar attempt to reconcile both positions, Schadow (2013, 298–9) has argued that we need to understand (intellectualist) moral consciousness and (affectivist) moral feeling as two aspects of the same moral motivation, understood in terms of a determination of the will by the moral law. Ware (2014, 742), in turn, has argued that "neither the intellectualist nor the affectivist views give us the resources we need to understand Kant's unique kind of phenomenology in the second *Critique*." Instead, Ware (2014, 742–3) argues that we need to distinguish between a first and a third-person perspective. He criticizes intellectualism for claiming that "our recognition of the moral law is a sufficient condition for moral motivation," and opposes McCarty's affectivism for considering "the question of moral motivation from a third-person perspective." From the perspective of Kant's general conception of feeling, Cohen (2018, 18–19 n.) has argued convincingly against affectivism and intellectualism for ignoring Kant's category of a "rational feeling," to which the moral feeling of respect belongs: "As such ... it functions neither as an inclination, as affectivists believe, nor as a cognition, as intellectualists believe; rather, it has the unique features of a rational feeling insofar as it manifests the conditions of moral agency."

Berg (2021, 740) has proposed an alternative account beyond intellectualism and affectivism, arguing for "the *identity* of the conscious determination of the will by the law," which represents intellectualism, "and the feeling of moral respect," which represents affectivism. I shall call this Berg's "Identity Thesis" about intellectualism and affectivism. According to this thesis, "Kant is able to derive the feeling of moral respect *a priori* and no wedge can be driven between the determination of one's will and the feeling of moral respect" (2021, 748). According to Berg's Identity Thesis, moral respect "*just is* the immediate, conscious determination of the will by the moral law." However, Berg's Identity Thesis does not consider the causal relationship between the moral law and the moral feeling of respect, to which Kant refers in many places (e.g. 4:401 n.; 5:73; 5:75). The moral feeling of respect is not *identical* to the will's determination by the moral law but rather its *consequence*. Berg further claims that "there is no conceptual gap between recognizing the authority of the moral law and acting morally that ought to be filled by an extra motivating element" (Berg 2021, 741). This leads her to the conclusion that "[f]eeling – intrinsic to the function of a finite rational will – rather than being a hindrance to our freedom, is its embodiment" (Berg 2021, 757).

As convincing as Berg's attempt "to dispel the suspicion that Kant's practical philosophy is grounded in an unacceptable dualism" (Berg 2021, 757) is, she does not consider the larger transcendental framework of Kant's conception of autonomy, nor does she consider the complexity of the will itself that is at issue here. Accordingly, the Identity Thesis is problematic in that it identifies normative entities, such as the moral law, with descriptive entities, such as feeling, too quickly. Furthermore, the Identity Thesis cannot explain how we can cultivate moral respect in terms of education, and how we can be *responsible* for cultivating respect. Against the Identity Thesis of moral respect, the volitionalist approach that I shall propose allows distinguishing between various forms of causation of the moral law and mediating between reason and sensibility, without identifying them immediately. Instead, the volitionalist account considers the moral feeling of respect as part of the human will's causal formation of autonomy. Furthermore, the Identity Thesis implies determinism about moral respect that is at odds with Kant's claim that we still need the faculty of choice to incorporate respect into our maxim to act morally and imputably. For otherwise the determination by moral respect would lead to what the early post-Kantian debate on freedom of the will has called "intelligible fatalism" (Schmid 1790).

In what follows, I shall agree with Berg, Cohen, Frierson, Schadow and Ware that we need to go beyond affectivism and intellectualism to properly understand Kant's theses about moral respect. However, I shall do so not by distinguishing between different perspectives, be they transcendental or personal, but by referring to Kant's complex notion of will. I shall argue for a volitionalist account that allows doing justice to both affectivist and intellectualist approaches, and which can be integrated into Kant's larger conception of autonomy.[46] In a central passage in his second *Critique*, Kant proposes his Rationality Thesis, according to which "[t]he feeling [of respect] ... is not pathological, as would be a feeling produced by an object of the senses, but practical only, that is, possible through a preceding (objective) determination of the will and causality of reason" (5:80). Furthermore, at various points in his work, Kant speaks of moral respect in causal terms. This causation is not to be confused with empirical causation happening in time and space, as respect is not subject to the category of causality of our understanding. Rather, it is the effect

---

[46] Frankfurt (1994, 434) has provided a volitionalist interpretation of love, which "is neither affective nor cognitive" but "volitional." However, opposed to my volitionalist account of respect, Frankfurt's volitionalist account of love does not allow interpreting love as a unified account to which also affective and cognitive aspects belong. I agree with Frankfurt that the notion of autonomy is of special importance for the volitionalist account. However, opposed to his account (1994, 435), I am especially interested in the relationship between autonomy, reason, morality, and imputability.

of an intelligible causality of freedom. Although moral respect is not caused empirically, it has empirical manifestations concerning events in inner sense.

Ware (2014, 742) has argued with regard to moral respect that "there is little we can say about causal relations beyond the sphere of possible experience." To overcome the dualism between affectivism and intellectualism, he proposes a distinction between a third-person and a first-person perspective: "Kant is bracketing the question of reason's causal efficacy, from a third-person perspective, focusing instead on the question of what the moral law must feel like, from a first-person perspective" (2014, 734). However, this is true only from a theoretical but not from a practical point of view. Whereas from a theoretical point of view we cannot understand the transition from the intelligible to the sensible due to lacking intuition, this is possible from a practical point of view, because the will serves as a kind of mediation, being determinable both rationally and empirically. Kant explicitly argues that in case of the moral feeling of respect, "we can see a priori that the moral law, as the determining ground of the will, must by thwarting all our inclinations produce a feeling that can be called pain" (5:73) and that "we have the first and perhaps the only case in which we can determine a priori from concepts the relation of a cognition (here the cognition of a pure practical reason) to the feeling of pleasure or displeasure" (5:73). Furthermore, Kant proposes the Rationality Thesis that "this feeling is the only one that we can cognize completely a priori and the necessity of which we can have insight into" (5:73). Likewise, Kant claims that respect is "a feeling that is positive in its intellectual cause, which is known a priori" (5:79)

Looking back at the second *Critique*, Kant in his third *Critique* argues that "we actually derived the feeling of respect (as a special and peculiar modification of this feeling, which will not coincide exactly either with the pleasure or with the displeasure that we obtain from empirical objects) from universal moral concepts a priori." He even goes on arguing that "there we could also step beyond the bounds of experience and appeal to a causality that rests on a supersensible property of the subject, namely that of freedom" (5:222). This transition from the noumenal to the empirical, which the moral feeling of respect marks, is what Kant calls the idea of freedom, which "has its place solely in the relation of the intellectual, as cause, to the appearance, as effect" (4:344). However, from a volitionalist point of view, the transition of respect is not mysterious at all, because it happens within the human faculties of the mind.[47]

---

[47] For a discussion of this transition, without considering a volitionalist interpretation, see Lauener (1981, 253).

4.3 Compatibilism about Respect

In many places, Kant speaks of respect in terms of causality, which he further explains in terms of an effect of noumenal causality. This causal reading of respect allows connecting it to Kant's notion of the will. According to Kant's Rationality Thesis, the moral feeling of respect is "*self-wrought* by means of a rational concept" (4:401 n.), and it is "produced ... through a preceding (objective) determination of the will and causality of reason" (5:80), namely by "the lawgiving of practical reason" (5:92), so that it is not "pathologically" but "practically effected" (5:75) and caused by the "influence of a mere intellectual idea on feeling" (5:80). As we saw in Section 2, the ascription of moral respect "presuppose[s] a limitation of the nature of a being" (5:79), that is, a finite rational being such as human beings are. In this section, therefore, I shall discuss moral respect in light of Kant's moral anthropology that is grounded in Kant's transcendental philosophy, especially his distinction between the intelligible and the sensible character, which I will apply to the complex structure of the human will.

Whereas interpreters have tried to make sense of respect's special status by isolating it from its conceptual context and merely focusing on its role in moral motivation,[48] I shall focus on the systematic position of the moral feeling of respect within the framework of Kant's conception of moral autonomy, and ground it in Kant's conception of self-reflective will. This calls for referring to Kant's transcendental distinction between the intelligible and empirical character, given that moral respect is finally grounded in this distinction, which can be applied to the human will. Kant describes the human will as standing "between its a priori principle, which is formal, and its a posteriori incentive, which is material, as at a crossroads" (4:400). According to this double-aspect theory, the human will can be determined both empirically, by the law of nature, and by the moral law, that is pure practical reason. In each case it is the same will, albeit distinguished in the lower and the higher appetitive faculty (5:25). In opposition to both the intellectualist and the affectivist view, the volitionalist interpretation of respect yields the reality of freedom by demonstrating its unity, without dividing the subject into a rational and sensible part as the ontological two-world interpretation seems to suggest, and without referring to the epistemological two-standpoints interpretation that cannot do justice to the reality and phenomenology of moral respect.[49]

---

[48] See McCarty (1993, 434), who, in his own words, has "tried to elucidate here the role Kant supposes it plays in moral motivation, but ... not attempted any explanation of its etiology or phenomenology."

[49] See Frierson (2010, 84): "[T]wo-standpoint theories seem to lack a suitable answer to the question of whether human beings are *really* free."

According to the volitional compatibilist account, the "intellectualist" and the "affectivist" views can be reconciled. Such a compatibilist view does not conceive of the moral feeling of respect in terms of a mechanical model (as the German word "Triebfeder" – "driving force" – may suggest) but as a process of the subject's moral formation, that is, as a process of moral self-consciousness and moral autonomy.[50] I shall argue that moral respect is a kind of practical cognition that entails epistemological, motivational, and phenomenological dimensions. In doing so, I will argue for an internalist account, according to which respect is a special self-reflective volitional structure of a rational agent being morally motivated by a moral judgment.[51] According to this view, Kant's concept of moral respect demonstrates the unity of such a self-reflective will by uniting rational and emotional states in the course of the agent's moral self-formation, which includes all three human faculties of the mind.

Kant's theory of moral respect is grounded in a fundamental theme common to all three *Critiques,* namely the distinction between things-in-themselves and appearances. The transition from the former to the latter designates the realm of freedom, or as Kant puts it: "The idea of freedom has its place solely in the relation of the intellectual, as cause, to the appearance, as effect" (4:344). In his third *Critique,* Kant stresses the idea of freedom with regard to its epistemological status which is "the only one among all the ideas of pure reason whose object is a *fact* and which must be counted among the *scibilia*"[52] (5:468). Therefore, we need to discuss the transcendental framework of moral respect in terms of what Kant calls a "causality of reason" and a "causality of freedom."

However, we first need to discuss how to understand Kant's statements about the ontological status of the sensible (phenomenal) and intelligible (noumenal) natures or "worlds."[53] McCarty (2009, xv) has argued that "Kant combined freedom and psychological determinism through his assumption that we act in two worlds, literally." The ontological two-worlds interpretation entails that human beings are free insofar as they exist in a noumenal world of things-in-

---

[50] Ware (2014, 728) has stressed the importance of reading Kant's conception "from the agent's own point of view." However, Ware does not consider the special volitional structure that goes along with this agent-oriented view. In line with my volitionalist reading of the moral feeling of respect, Engstrom (2010, 92) has argued that "the mechanistic meaning itself rests on a more basic biological idea of an inner driving force."

[51] Allison (1990, 122) has pointed out that "it is the consciousness of the law, not the law itself, that functions as the actual moral incentive." However, he does not discuss the role of will in detail. Melissa Zinkin (2006, 35) has emphasized this volitional structure of respect. See also Berg (2021, 741) and Schadow (2013, 298–9). Guevara (2000, 97) argues that respect's nature is "both cognitive and conative."

[52] Latin for "things that can be known."

[53] See Watkins (2005, 317), who raises the question "whether the distinction between appearances and things-in-themselves is epistemological (sometimes called methodological) or rather ontological."

themselves and determined insofar as they exist in a phenomenal world of mere appearances. According to the epistemological two-aspects-interpretation, however, whether we are free (from the practical standpoint of the faculty of pure practical reason) or determined (from the theoretical standpoint of the faculty of understanding) depends on the point of view.[54] Yet how can we conceive of the sensible and the rational to better understand the features of the moral feeling of respect?

According to Kant's first *Critique*, each realm has to be conceived of as governed and structured by special laws. The intelligible realm stands under the law of freedom while the sensible realm is governed by the law of nature, with the latter being structured by time and space and the former existing outside of any spatial and temporal relations. Insofar as we are members of the realm of sense, our choices and actions fall under the laws of nature. However, insofar as we are members of the realm of reason, we are free and thus our wills are governed by the moral law. In what follows, I shall argue for an interpretation beyond the strong two-world and the weak two-aspect interpretation, referring to Kant's complex notion of the will.

In his *Groundwork*, Kant refers to respect in terms of a volitional structure by distinguishing between an objective and a subjective determining ground of the will. The objective determining ground is what Kant calls "the practical *law*" (4:401 n.). This objective determination of the will by the pure *form* of the moral law can be interpreted in terms of formal causation (see Section 2.2). Moral respect, according to this volitional distinction, is a special volitional phenomenon that is closely linked to Kant's notion of a maxim as "the subjective principle of volition" (4:401 n.). However, in contrast to Zinkin (2006, 36 n.), who argues that the "subjective determination of the will ... should be understood in the sense of what Kant will later refer to as 'Willkür', the power of choice," I will argue that the subjective determination of the will, as moral respect, is not to be confused with moral choice in the strict sense, which also implies a choice of what is morally evil. This idea is supported by a passage in the *Groundwork* footnote:[55] "What I cognize immediately as a law for me I cognize with respect, which signifies merely consciousness of the subordination of my will to a law without the mediation of other influences on my sense" (4:401 n.). The subordination of my will to the moral law is indeed moral autonomy but not identical to moral *choice*, which is necessary for an action to be fully imputable. Kant stresses in his *Religion* that "the free power of choice

---

[54] See Allison (1983, 239). For a discussion of both approaches regarding moral freedom, see Frierson (2010).

[55] I thank the anonymous reviewers for drawing my attention to the problem of respect and moral choice.

incorporates moral feeling into its maxim" so that "[t]he subjective ground ... of our incorporating this incentive into our maxims seems to be an addition to personality" (6:27–8).

4.4 The Causality of Respect

According to Kant's account of human action, both kinds of causality – causality of nature and causality of reason – must be conceived as "*necessarily united* in the same subject" (4:456). This means that "we could calculate a human being's conduct for the future with as much certainty as a lunar or solar eclipse and could nevertheless maintain that the human being's conduct is free" (5:99). Kant describes such a kind of rational causality as a "causality of freedom" or as "absolute spontaneity of causes," and also as "transcendental freedom" (B 474). He notes – already anticipating his *Critique of Practical Reason* – that it "is especially noteworthy that it is the transcendental idea of freedom on which the practical concept of freedom is grounded" (B 561). The transcendental concept of an absolute spontaneity grounds the *practical* spontaneity in the sense of practical freedom, which is "that freedom in which reason has causality in accordance with objective determining grounds" (4:346). As such, the transcendental idea of freedom in the sense of an "absolute spontaneity of an action" constitutes "the real ground of its imputability" (B 476).

However, the volitionalist account of moral respect does not only allow grounding it within Kant's transcendental idealism but also understanding it in terms of feeling. In his third *Critique,* Kant, looking back at the second *Critique*, argues that "we did not actually derive this feeling [of respect] from the idea of the moral as a cause, rather it was merely the determination of the will that was derived from the latter" (5:222). This passage supports the volitionalist account, since "[t]he state of mind of a will determined by something, however, is in itself already a feeling of pleasure and is identical with it" (5:222).[56] Therefore, referring to Kant's notion of will allows us to understand respect both in terms of a feeling, as the affectivists do, and as an intelligible cause, as the intellectualists do.

5 Reason's Self-Consciousness: The Autonomy of Respect

Having argued for a volitionalist interpretation beyond intellectualism and affectivism in the previous section, in this section I will interpret moral respect more precisely in terms of the self-consciousness of moral autonomy.[57] This

---

[56] Berg (2021, 740) has pointed to this "usually overlook[ed]" passage.
[57] For a discussion of the moral feeling of respect with regard to autonomy, see Allison (1990, 125–6). However, Allison does not discuss the role of moral self-consciousness for moral respect.

reading is supported by Kant's claim that respect is both the "[i]mmediate determination of the will by means of the law" and at the same time "consciousness of this" (4:401 n.). The notion of respect is related to that of autonomy in that it allows us to understand how it *feels* from a first-person perspective to be autonomous, which implies being morally motivated. In other words, the moral feeling of respect is the answer to the question, "What is it like to be autonomous?" As such, it does not only concern the will as being determined by the moral law from a third-person perspective but also the consciousness of a will being self-determined by the moral law from a first-person perspective. In his *Religion*, Kant argues that "respect for the law, which in its subjective aspect is called moral feeling, is identical with consciousness of one's duty" (6:464). Accordingly, the moral feeling of respect concerns the executive dimension of morality, as Kant argues in his Mrongovius notes in terms of autocracy:

> If reason determines the will through the moral law, it has the force of an incentive, and in that case has, not autonomy merely, but also autocracy. It then has both legislative and executive power. The autocracy of reason, to determine the will in accordance with moral laws, would then be the moral feeling. (29:626)

Kant argues in his *Metaphysics of Morals* that "any consciousness of obligation depends upon moral feeling" (6:399). He discusses moral respect in terms of "self-knowledge" (5:86) with regard to the problem of self-conceit and self-love. According to the volitionalist interpretation, respect is a process of moral motivation in terms of volitional moral self-consciousness. We can only feel respect toward "what is connected with my will merely as ground and never as effect" (4:401). In the previous section, I have argued that the will is grounded in pure practical reason and can be understood in terms of a causality of reason. However, moral respect, according to Kant, is structurally self-reflective in terms of the self-consciousness of a morally autonomous being. Kant claims that the moral feeling of respect is "nothing other than the sensation of the determinability of the will through reason itself" (20:207). This self-reflexivity allows addressing the Rationality Thesis, the Subjectivity Thesis, and the Intentionality Thesis.

5.1 The Intentionality of Respect

From a causal point of view, an autonomous will, as Kant conceives it, can be determined "objectively [by] the *law* and subjectively [by] *pure respect* for this practical law" (4:400). The subjective determination of the will is no additional determination by an extra factor but rather the self-reflective version of the objective determination. Kant does not argue that the moral law as such determines the will but rather its *"representation"* (*Vorstellung*) (4:401). This representation of the moral law can be better understood by referring to the concept of feeling. Kant argues that feeling, generally understood, "is the effect of a representation (that may be either sensible or intellectual) upon a subject and belongs to sensibility, even though the representation itself may belong to the understanding or to reason)" (6:211). Since practical reason is the faculty of desire (5:198), it follows that a representation of the pure will, that is of pure practical reason, can also be felt. Respect, as Kant puts it, is "properly the representation of a worth that infringes upon my self-love" (4:401 n.), and it "depends on the representation of a law only as to its form and not on account of any object of the law" (5:80).

We can interpret this self-consciousness in terms of autonomy of the will. Along these lines, Kant argues that "[t]he consciousness of a free submission of the will to the law, yet as combined with an unavoidable constraint put on all inclinations though only by one's own reason, is respect for the law" (5:80). This quotation entails Kant's very idea of autonomy. In the *Groundwork* footnote, Kant further argues that "[t]he *object* of respect is ... simply the *law*, and indeed the law that we impose upon *ourselves* and yet as necessary in itself. ... [A]s imposed upon us by ourselves it is nevertheless a result of our will" (4:401 n.). The moral law is insofar a "result" of our will as we reflect it volitionally and thereby endorse it. However, it is not a result of our will in so far as we bring it about. Therefore, the moral law is both the cause *and*, as the "result," a kind of effect of the autonomous will. This causal closure describes Kant's conception of the autonomy of the will. It shows that the intentionality of moral respect is rather complex and needs to be understood in light of Kant's conception of autonomy.

In his *Groundwork*, Kant defines autonomy of the will as "the property of the will by which it is a law to itself.... The principle of autonomy is, therefore: to choose only in such a way that the maxims of your choice (*Wahl*) are also included as universal law in the same volition" (4:440). As the Cambridge translation of this passage points out, Kant does not use the word "Willkür," which he more frequently uses in his *Religion* and in his *Metaphysics of Morals*, to distinguish it from the notion of will (6:226), but only the German word "Wahl" to characterize his notion of autonomy. Accordingly, autonomy of the will is not about moral choice in the broader sense, as a choice between good or evil maxims, but rather a choice of *only* morally good maxims. This, however, raises the question of how to understand moral respect from the perspective of moral imputability, which I will discuss in Section 8.

Interpreting moral respect according to the volitionalist account in terms of autonomy allows us to tackle Kant's Intentionality Thesis, and to further analyze the second-person perspective of respect. Kant describes moral respect as being directed toward various possible intentional objects: (i) to persons that constitute a moral example;[58] (ii) to the moral law;[59] (iii) to ourselves as moral persons.[60] How these intentional objects are to be related is controversial in research. Massey (1983, 63) distinguishes between "reverence for actually moral people and respect for potentially moral people" and argues that "reverence for the moral law provides the basis for both of them." Theis (2005, 346) distinguishes only between respect for the law and respect for the person and claims that "it is through respect for the person that the necessity of, and hence respect for, the law is established." Merritt (2018, 57) argues that "Kant treats respect for the moral law as the genus under which distinct species of respect for particular persons – recognition respect and esteem respect – can be determined." Against Massey, Theis, and Merritt, I shall argue that it is self-respect that allows understanding the unity of respect's intentionality in terms of moral autonomy. According to the volitionalist account, self-respect in terms of moral autonomy means that the will is not only determined by the moral law (5:71) such that the moral law *forms* and *directs* its volitions but that the will recognizes the moral law as its *own* law and therefore *authorizes* its volitions.

Walschots (2022, 257) distinguishes between "three main objects" of moral respect: (i) "the moral law"; (ii) "persons insofar as they exemplify the moral law"; (iii) "persons simply insofar as they are persons or ends-in-themselves." Whereas I agree with Walschots's distinction between (i), (ii), and (iii), I shall argue that this distinction as such does not fully take into account the intentional self-reflexivity and dynamics of moral respect that allows understanding it in terms of moral autonomy. What is important about these forms of intentionality is that they are not merely cognitive but rather volitional. The threefold intentionality does not mean, however, that the three intentional objects of moral respect are distinct from each other. Rather, these objects appear in various stages and contexts of moral self-consciousness, understood in terms of moral autonomy. In Section 8, I shall discuss these stages from the perspective of moral cultivation and education.

Initially, moral respect is directed to human individuals that are involved in contexts of moral action. However, Kant emphasizes that respect is not directed to human beings, because "[a] human being," understood as an empirical subject with individual qualities such as "jocular humor," "courage and strength," and "power he has by his rank among others" can indeed "be an object of my love, fear, or admiration even to amazement and yet not be an object of respect" (5:77).

---

[58] E.g. 5:76–7; 5:81n.   [59] E.g. 4:400; 5:78; 5:128; 5:132; 6:464.
[60] E.g. 5:93; 5:161; 5:257; 5:257.

Here, Kant refers to his *Groundwork* (4:393) where he had distinguished various kinds of relative values that human beings possess and exemplify, such as "*talents* of mind," "qualities of *temperament*," and "*gifts of fortune*," and which he distinguished from the absolute value of the goodwill. Kant therefore argues that "strictly speaking," the respect "which we show to ... a person" is actually respect "to the law that his example holds before us" (5:78). To motivate us, the moral law does not appear as an abstract object but needs to be "made intuitive by an example" (5:77). Therefore, in respecting another person, we are not directed to the "natural constitution of an organized being" (4:395) but to its moral constitution as a rational being. Kant argues that our "highest respect" is directed toward what he calls our "*personality*," that is, the "freedom and independence from the mechanism of the whole of nature, regarded nevertheless as also a capacity of a being subject to special laws – namely pure practical laws given by his own reason" (5:87). At the same time, a person as an "*end in itself*" need not necessarily be understood as a *morally* acting person in order to be respected but rather as a subject *capable* of acting morally, that is, as a "*subject of the moral law*" (5:131, see 5:87). For, as I shall argue in Section 8.2, we must respect even persons who act immorally.

So far, the moral law is presented as something external to us that we recognize – be it instantiated and mediated by another person or be it the moral law *itself*. This, however, does not allow for moral motivation and autonomy, since it would be compatible with an empirically caused feeling such as fear. Moreover, due to our propensity for self-conceit, moral respect toward another person can be experienced as a burdensome feeling, since "we give way to it only reluctantly with regard to a human being," as Kant puts it: "We try to discover something that could lighten the burden of it for us, some fault in him to compensate us for the humiliation that comes upon us through such an example" (577). Our propensity for self-conceit consists in the attempt to argue, by means of reason, against the demand of the moral law, that is to *abuse* reason. Rationalizing means finding reasons to justify one's individual interests as being exempt from the demands of the moral law, that is, "to cast doubt upon their validity, or at least upon their purity and strictness, and, where possible, to make them better suited to our wishes and inclinations, that is, to corrupt them" (4:407). Therefore, rationalizing ultimately leads to an *incapacity* to feel and cultivate moral respect toward other persons.

Kant further argues that "[t]he majesty of the law ... instills awe," and distinguishes this effect from "dread, which repels." However, with regard to moral autonomy, "this awe rouses the respect of the subject toward his master, except that in this case, since the master lies in us, it rouses a *feeling of the sublimity* of our own vocation" (6:23 n.). Recognizing ourselves not only as objects but also *subjects* of moral respect is what Kant calls "*respect for ourselves* in the consciousness of our freedom" (5:161).

To act out of duty, and to avoid mere moral legality, the objective moral law has to become internal and self-reflective – a kind of moral self-recognition. Kant argues in line with Walschots's (iii) when he writes that "[o]ur own will insofar as it would act only under the condition of a possible giving of universal law through its maxims ... is *the proper object of respect*" (4:440; emphasis mine). If we understand moral respect in terms of autonomy and of a self-reflective will, it becomes obvious that the intentionality of self-respect (iii) is compatible with (i) and (ii) since it is not directed toward a human individual but to a possible subject of the moral law. Kant calls this form the "the idea of humanity in our subject" (5:257) and "respect for the dignity of humanity in our own person" (5:273). Likewise, "self-esteem" is actually directed to "the humanity within us" (5:335). Self-respect is distinguished from (i) and (ii) due to being the very condition for any other form of respect and also of duty.[61] Kant argues that a person "must have respect for the law within himself in order even to think of any duty whatsoever" (6:403). I will discuss the normative implications of self-respect for our duties in Section 8.

Kant emphasizes, however, that the moral autonomy of respect must not be understood in terms of individual persons referring to themselves. Instead, he points out that if the obligator and the obligated person were identical as an individual, the obligator could arbitrarily absolve the latter from the obligation or even abolish the moral law altogether. This can only be avoided if not an individual person but humanity in our person, understood in terms of pure practical reason and its imperative to universalize, is lawgiving (23:400–1).

In light of the intentionality of self-respect, Kant's Subjectivity Thesis, according to which "respect for the law is not the incentive to morality; instead, it is morality itself subjectively considered as an incentive" (5:76), can be understood more precisely. In the following Sections 5.2 and 5.3, I shall argue that from a volitional point of view, moral respect is not only determined by the objective moral law, but *is also the activity of a will* that reflects on the moral law and thereby gives itself the moral law by subjectively endorsing it. This again points to the close relationship between moral respect and moral autonomy.

---

[61] Accordingly, I agree with Sensen (2013a, 35) that "[f]or Kant obligations arise from the first-personal standpoint, not the second-personal." However, this standpoint is only a first step toward moral self-consciousness. In order to act out of duty, we must not remain at the first-personal standpoint but rise to a universal standpoint.

5.2 The Autonomy of Respect

To better understand the autonomous intentionality of moral respect, we need to consider Kant's notion of autonomy in general. Sensen (2013b, 2) has put the problem of autonomy as follows: "Does Kant's conception refer to the legislation of empirical persons, of pure reason, or of a specific kind of principles?" Since Kant conceives of freedom as a causality of reason, we can interpret it in terms of the moral law. However, as Karl Ameriks (2013, 54) has pointed out, there are several "ambiguities" that concern "the provocative nature of Kant's self-legislative characterization of autonomy." According to Ameriks, we must avoid both an existentialist interpretation, according to which autonomy means purely individual self-determination without any reference to moral normativity, and an interpretation that conceives of autonomy in terms of a "wholly transcendent 'metaphysical self'" (Ameriks 2013, 53), which has no connection to the individual person and her actions in the sensible world. In any case, to do justice to Kant's account of autonomy, and to tackle Kant's Intentionality Thesis, we need to distinguish between a cognitive or rational aspect of autonomy and a causal aspect, as Reath (2013, 49) has pointed out. Therefore, we need to understand how the cognitive and the causal aspects of autonomy are related to moral respect.

Kant explains the complex relationship between freedom and the moral law as follows: the moral law is the epistemic condition of freedom of the will, its *ratio cognoscendi*, and freedom of the will the ontological condition of the moral law, its *ratio essendi* (5:4). He associates this law with a specific concept of causality, which he calls "causality through freedom" or "causality of reason" (4:458; B 579; 5:80; 5:475) in contrast to natural causality. Kant's conception of freedom of the will is deeply linked to this special kind of causality. According to Kant, there is a fundamental asymmetry between the two types of determination and laws. Unlike natural causality, the causality of reason does not affect the will from "outside," that is, it does not determine the will heteronomously, but unfolds its power of determination from the generally reasonable nature of pure will itself, which, in contrast to a "lower faculty of desire" (*unteres Begehrungsvermögen*) that is determined by material determinants, is distinguished as an "upper faculty of desire (*oberes Begehrungsvermögen*)." Ameriks (2013, 69) has therefore argued that "the authorial self surely must be not a particular individual as such, but the faculty of reason in general ..., and in a general sense that is not limited to the human species." By virtue of the determination by pure reason, the will becomes what Kant calls a "causality of freedom," which is realized as an action. The will, as Kant puts it, "is a kind of causality of living beings insofar as they are rational, and freedom would be that property of such causality that it can be efficient independently of alien causes determining it" (4:446).

But how can we understand the form of the law of reason that determines the positive concept of freedom of will? Kant has closely linked his metaphysical theory of the autonomous will as a causality of freedom to his normative theory of human morality. For Kant, absolute freedom of will is freedom in view of the normativity of morality. The will gives itself a law that essentially its *own* law (4:431). However, not only the act of self-legislation, but at the same time, the reflection and identification of the law, which make it recognizable as a *self-imposed* law, are constitutive elements of rational freedom. Thereby, Kant claims that the autonomous person "is subject only to laws given by himself but still universal" (4:432).

5.3 The Logic of Respect

Kant's conception of autonomy is systematically outlined in the "Analytic of pure practical reason" of his second *Critique*. There, Kant relates the structure of autonomy to the structure of his first *Critique*. He argues that "the order in the subdivision of the Analytic" is "the reverse of that in the *Critique* of pure speculative reason" (5:16). In the Transcendental doctrine of elements in the first *Critique*, Kant first discussed the role of the senses and intuition in the Transcendental aesthetic, then proceeded to the Transcendental logic, including the Analytic of concepts, and finally dealt with the Analytic of principles. By contrast, in the Analytic of pure practical reason of his second *Critique* Kant begins "with *principles* and proceed[s] to *concepts,* and only then, where possible, from them to the senses" (5:16). In fact, what Kant means by the "senses" is the moral feeling of respect, whereby "sensibility is not regarded as a capacity for intuition at all but only as feeling" (5:90).

Structurally, the Analytic has the form of a syllogism, "proceeding from the universal in the major premise (the moral principle), through undertaking in a minor premise a subsumption of possible actions (as good or evil) under the former, to the conclusion, namely, the subjective determination of the will (an interest in the practically possible good and in the maxim based on it)" (5:90). In his first *Critique*, Kant generally defines a syllogism as follows: "In every syllogism I think first a *rule* (the *major*) through the understanding. Second, I *subsume* a cognition under the condition of the rule (the minor) by means of the *power of judgment*. Finally, I determine my cognition through the predicate of the rule (the *conclusio*), hence *a priori* through *reason*" (B 360–1). This shows that all three faculties of the human mind are involved in a syllogism, and that to understand moral respect, we need to consider the complex interplay between these faculties and their respective roles and limits. This interplay further illustrates the compatibilist volitionalist account of moral respect, according to which the "intellectualist" and the "affectivist" views can be reconciled. Moral respect is a process of the subject's moral formation, that is, a process of moral self-consciousness and moral autonomy, which Kant describes in terms of a syllogism of pure practical reason.

In the syllogism of pure practical reason, the conclusion, which Kant calls a subjective moral "interest" (5:90), expresses the moral feeling of respect. Likewise, Kant identifies moral respect with the self-reflection of autonomy, namely with "[t]he consciousness of a *free* submission of the will to the law, yet as combined with an unavoidable constraint put on all inclinations though only by one's own reason" (5:80). From a third-person perspective, I shall call this practical syllogism the "logic of respect." However, the "deduction" of moral respect is not analytical but synthetic, because it depends on the moral law as a premise that can be cognized a priori as the "fact of reason," which "forces itself upon us of itself as a synthetic a priori proposition that is not based on any intuition" (5:31). Therefore, the moral feeling of respect is not a theoretical intellectual intuition, but an a priori practical determination and self-reflection of the will that can be described from a third- and first-person perspective.

In analogy to a rational syllogism, practical reason can be grouped into three stations of its formation of a causality of freedom.[62] What is special about this syllogism of pure practical reason is that the conclusion is not merely deduced from conditioned premises, as it is in case of a theoretical syllogism, but causally *produced* by something unconditioned, namely the moral law itself, which, as Kant points out in his *Groundwork*, is "an a priori synthetic practical proposition" (4:420). This practical syllogism must therefore be understood as a form of practical knowledge and self-consciousness, that is, as an a priori volitional structure whose different logical steps together constitute a causality of freedom. The conclusion of the syllogism of pure practical reason is therefore not a merely logical conclusion but a volitional production (5:76). In Chapter II of his analytic of practical reason, Kant, confirming the volitionalist reading of respect, writes that

> since all precepts of pure practical reason have to do only with the *determination of the will*, ... the practical a priori concepts in relation to the supreme principle of freedom at once become cognitions and do not have to wait for intuitions in order to receive meaning; and this happens for the noteworthy reason that they themselves produce the reality of that to which they refer (the disposition of the will), which is not the business of theoretical concepts. (5:66)

---

[62] For the systematic importance of this syllogism for Kant's notion of respect in 5:75, see Metz (2004, 142). However, Metz neither interprets this syllogism in causal terms regarding the notion of will nor discusses the relationship between respect and autonomy extensively.

Kant summarizes the causal and productive function of the moral law as follows:

> [T]he moral law, since it is a *formal determining ground* of action through practical pure reason and since it is also a material but only *objective determining ground* of the objects of action under the name of good and evil, is also a *subjective determining ground* – that is, an incentive – to this action inasmuch as it has influence on the sensibility of the subject and effects a feeling conducive to the influence of the law upon the will. (5:75; emphasis mine)

Here, the question arises of how to understand respect's being "conducive to the influence of the law upon the will." With regard to this question, I shall distinguish between determinists and electivists. Whereas determinists argue that moral respect is *sufficient* for moral action, electivists argue that we need additional *choice* for realizing a moral action.

6 Avoiding Self-Conceit: The Impact of Respect

As I have argued in the previous section, respect is not just a static theoretical attitude but rather a dynamic self-referential volitional process of moral autonomy, and it can also be understood in terms of a feeling. This process manifests on various levels both in terms of human faculties and moral phenomenology. According to Kant's Intentionality Thesis, the "self" of moral self-consciousness is not an empirical and individual self, but a universal moral self, which Kant calls "*humanity*" (5:87). Indeed, this does not mean that when we are morally self-conscious, we are fused into a group mind. Rather, we are not concerned with our individual interests but with interests that are universalizable in terms of the categorical imperative and its universal law (4:421; 5:30). Therefore, moral respect "is to be understood as the *maxim* of limiting our self-esteem by the dignity of humanity in another person" (6:449).

Here, however, the question is how empirical individuality comes into play. Kant applies the transcendental distinction between appearances and things-in-themselves developed in his *Critique of Pure Reason* to the twofold nature of human beings and the human will. As finite sensible beings, we are "so constituted that the matter of the faculty of desire (objects of inclination, whether of hope or fear) first forces itself upon us" (5:74). Human beings are both sensible and rational, and their will can be determined by both inclinations and pure practical reason, which demands that they need to be motivated to moral action. Hence, the moral feeling of respect has the function of a moral incentive that transforms mere legality to morality. What is important for moral motivation is the "distinction between consciousness of having acted *in conformity with duty* and *from duty*," whereby Kant identifies the latter with "respect for the law" (5:81).

6.1 Conflict, Scale, or Justification?

Kant's conception of rational moral motivation is complex, and moral respect portrays this complexity on various levels. At a first glance, the moral feeling of respect stands in opposition to merely natural feelings when it comes to the moral determination of the will, which leads to the autonomy of pure practical reason. There are three ways to understand this opposition: (i) as the internal conflict model between opposed forces and interests;[63] (ii) as the internal scale model;[64] and (iii) as the internal justification or judgment model.[65] Each model represents a special perspective on moral motivation, which depends on the perspective on human freedom.[66] The conflict model is based on an ideal, third-person perspective of pure practical reason, the scale model is based on a first-person spectator perspective, and the justification model on a first-person imputability perspective.[67]

From the ideal, third-person perspective of a causality of reason, as a capacity of freedom, the determination of will needs to exclude all heteronomous inclinations. The relationship between rational and empirical determining grounds is conceived as a kind of competition. Considered from this perspective, both possible determining grounds contend in the moral subject, as it were, for their decisive influence on the will, so as to translate their specific "interest" into an action. Kant thereby distinguishes between the interest of reason and of inclination in terms of "a principle that contains the condition under which alone its exercise is promoted." However, "[r]eason, as the faculty of principles, determines the interest of all the powers of the mind but itself determines its own" (5:119–20). Accordingly, pure practical reason, by determining itself with regard to the faculty of desire, also determines the interest of the power of judgment, and therefore our feeling of respect. Therefore, especially from a volitionalist point of view, we can discuss moral respect with regard to all human faculties of the mind.

---

[63] Allison (1990, 126) calls it the "conflict-of-forces conception of agency" and Ware (2014, 743) a "mechanical model of competing forces." However, neither distinguishes it from the scale model.
[64] Timmermann (2003, 204–7). [65] Reath (1989, 296–7), Allison (1990, 126–7).
[66] Buchheim (2001, 658) distinguishes between an ideal perspective on freedom that Kant supposes in his *Groundwork* and in his second *Critique*, and a factual individual perspective that Kant takes in his *Religion*.
[67] Ware (2014, 734) distinguishes between a (systematic) third-person and a (phenomenological) first-person perspective of moral motivation. However, he does not distinguish between a first-person spectator and a first-person imputability thesis. The first-person perspective that Ware addresses cannot explain the moral imputability of moral motivation. Respect in terms of freedom of choice needs to be discussed with regard to Kant's Normativity Thesis, which I will do in Section 8.

Kant distinguishes between the interest of "the sensible principle of happiness," which concerns the inclinations (5:120), and "the *moral interest*" as "a pure sense-free interest of practical reason alone" (5:79). Moral respect, as the moral law's subjective determining ground of the will, is "the capacity to take such an interest in the law" (5:80). According to the conflict model of moral motivation, virtue is "moral disposition *in conflict*" (5:84). Kant attributes both interests to a different subject. He calls the subject of moral respect "the subject of pure practical reason as the supreme lawgiver" (5:75) and connects it with the moral law, and opposes it to self-conceit, which he connects with "its subjective antagonist, namely the inclinations" (5:73). This conflict arises from Kant's normative demand that "when morality is in question, reason must not play the part of mere guardian to inclination but, disregarding it altogether, must attend solely to its own interest as pure practical reason" (5:118).

Within the conflict model of interest, Kant distinguishes between self-love and self-conceit, which are two forms of empirical interest. I will discuss self-love and self-conceit in more detail later, focusing here only on the role it plays for the conflict model. What is important for the conflict model is that Kant distinguishes between a weak and a strong kind of conflict between pure practical reason and regard for oneself. According to the weak conflict model, "[p]ure practical reason merely *infringes upon* self-love, inasmuch as it only restricts it, as natural and active in us even prior to the moral law, to the condition of agreement with this law, and then it is called *rational self-love*" (5:73).

In the *Groundwork* footnote discussed earlier, Kant had described the impact of respect from this perspective. There, he had defined respect as "the representation (*Vorstellung*) of a worth that infringes upon my self-love" (4:401 n.). According to the strong conflict model, however, respect "*strikes down* self-conceit altogether*" (5:73). Kant's conflict terminology of "infringing" (*Abbruch tun*) differs from "striking down" (*niederschlagen*) in crucial respects. Infringing self-love is compatible with the coexistence of self-love with respect for the moral law insofar self-love is subordinated and restricted, but not annihilated. Kant therefore says that pure practical reason "*merely* infringes upon self-love" (5:73; my emphasis), when he argues that self-love is restricted "to the condition of agreement with this law" and thereby being transformed to what Kant calls "*rational self-love*." This transformation model, however, does not hold in terms of self-conceit. For striking down self-conceit means that its claim is not only restricted but rather rejected, refuted, and therefore annihilated. In other words: there can be no agreement between the moral law and self-conceit.

However, the conflict model is problematic insofar as it suggests that the moral feeling of respect acts within the individual person without her volitional and imputable involvement. According to the conflict model, the moral person seems to be a mere spectator of her inner states, such as psychological forces and interests. Allison (1990, 126) has therefore criticized the conflict model from the perspective of individual freedom and electivism about respect, arguing that "inclinations do not determine the will in this manner." Rather, inclinations become practical "only by being 'incorporated into a maxim,' that is, by being taken by the agent (at least implicitly) as sufficient reasons for action."

According to the scale-model of moral motivation, the faculty of choice can be determined by rational and empirical motives in the quasi-mechanical model of a scale, whereby the counterweight to the inclinations must be maximized by pure practical reason, that is, by the weight of moral reasons, in order to tip to the moral side. The idea is that if we find enough *normative* reasons of pure practical reason, they will be the decisive factor in terms of a *motivating* reason. However, this cannot be done directly by placing normative reasons in one of two initially empty scales. Rather, Kant conceives of the scale as an initially asymmetrical state, according to which the scales tilt toward the inclinations. Following the metaphor of the scale model, inclinations and sensibility constitute an "obstacle to practical reason" (5:76) and its moral law, that is, an "internal obstacle [that] is opposed to it" (5:79). Therefore, in order to *strengthen* the scale pan of the moral law of pure practical reason, we need to *weaken* the scale pan of the inclinations by removing the obstacle. Kant says that "in the judgment of reason this removal of a hindrance is esteemed equivalent to a positive furthering of its causality" (5:75). However, Kant himself uses the mechanical terminology of a scale when he argues that "the relative weightiness of the law (with regard to a will affected by impulses), is produced in the judgment of reason through the removal of the counterweight" (5:76). Along these lines, Kant argues that "the lowering of pretensions to moral self-esteem – that is, humiliation on the sensible side – is an elevation of the moral – that is, practical – esteem for the law itself on the intellectual side" (5:79).

However, like the conflict model, the scale model suffers from severe problems, which become obvious if we adopt the first-person perspective of moral imputability. The problem with the metaphor of the scales is that the counterweight to practical reason is understood as an entirely *external* obstacle to reason, so that the empirical inclinations can only be understood as heteronomous influences, but not as possible reasons for a deliberative weighing process. Kant characterizes inclinations as "blind and servile" (5:118), which seems to imply that they are not volitional structures that can be imputed to us.[68] From the perspective of the scale model, only good, that is, *moral* reasons can be

---

[68] Reath (1989, 291) has criticized that according to the conflict model, "the idea that the subject's action stems ultimately from a choice made on the basis of reasons" is "missing."

consciously placed in the pan, whereas in the case of immoral actions we are, as it were, outweighed by inclinations. Therefore, Allison (1990, 126) has argued that in order to maintain moral imputability in moral motivation, we must show that "the spontaneity and rationality of the agent are involved even in heteronomous or inclination-based agency."

From the first-person perspective of moral imputability, the opposition between pure practical reason, self-love, and self-conceit must neither be understood in terms of a "conflict-of-forces conception of agency" nor as a scale model, but as a conflict "between two principles or standards of justification" (Allison 1990, 126–7). This interpretation focuses not on a conflict of forces or a mechanical movement but rather on the reasons, judgments, and justifications that become decisive for moral motivation. These reasons have been discussed in terms of normative and motivating reasons (Alvarez/Way 2024). According to this interpretation, inclinations are not to be conceived as forces but as principles of choice that can be understood in terms of a judgment, because "the faculty of desire" strives "to make *its claims* primary and originally valid" (5:74; emphasis mine).

6.2 Imputability about Respect

In order to argue for the first-person model of moral imputability, we need to further analyze what Kant calls self-love and self-conceit from the perspective of volitional judgment and justification. Kant's distinction between self-love and self-conceit implies a distinction between two volitional claims with regard to the moral law. He speaks of self-love and self-conceit in terms of a "propensity" (*Hang*) (5:74). What is important about a propensity is that it is imputable to an individual subject.[69] In his *Religion*, Kant defines a propensity as "the subjective ground of the possibility of an inclination ..., insofar as this possibility is contingent for humanity in general." As such, "[i]t is distinguished from a predisposition in that a propensity can indeed be innate yet *may* be represented as not being such: it can rather be thought of (if it is good) as *acquired*, or (if evil) as *brought* by the human being *upon* himself" (6:29).

However, Timmermann (2022, 103) has argued against Allison's incorporation thesis by pointing to the problem of moral failure. According to Timmermann, Allison endorses an intellectualist conception of moral choice, which cannot explain the possibility of immoral action because it conceives of it as a mere "cognitive error." In what follows, I will argue for a middle way between Allison and Timmermann concerning the imputability of immoral actions, which is also important for an understanding of respect beyond

---

[69] I agree with Ware (2014, 737) that "self-conceit involves an exercise of free choice – and so is something we are responsible for."

determinism and electivism. Thereby, I will focus on the volitional relationship between moral respect and self-conceit. I will argue that immoral action is not due to a lack of rationality but rather due to a misuse of rationality, which Kant explains in terms of rationalizing.

Self-conceit is not only a more intense form of self-love but differs from it in normative terms. Whereas self-love is a "propensity to make oneself as having subjective determining grounds of choice into the objective determining ground of the will," self-conceit "makes itself lawgiving and the unconditional practical principle" (5:74). Self-conceit is therefore the result of a normative reflection that falls prey to the moral error of confusing individual laws of the will with universal laws. It is, in other words, self-imposed heteronomy. In his *Metaphysics of Morals*, Kant defines "moral arrogance" as the "conviction of the greatness of one's moral worth, but only from failure to compare it with the law" (6:435). However, this moral failure is, like theoretical failure, imputable to the moral subject. Kant argues against a privative conception of moral and theoretical error (Noller 2021, 1469). Error cannot be traced back to a limitation or lack of our rational capacities, for "[i]n the restrictions of the understanding ... lies only the responsibility for ignorance; the responsibility for error we have to assign to ourselves" (9:54). We never err intentionally but always in the mode of self-incurred illusion so that the subject "confuses the illusion of truth with truth itself" (9:53). The impact of respect, from the perspective of the judgment model of moral motivation, is "an estimation of a worth that far outweighs any worth of what is recommended by inclination" (4:403). Regarding the "unconditional, incomparable worth" of the moral law, Kant therefore calls respect the only "expression for the estimate of it that a rational being must give" (4:436).

Although Kant uses mechanical metaphors throughout the chapter on the incentives of pure practical reason, not least that of an "incentive" (*Triebfeder*), which literally means a mechanical part of a clockwork, he also uses concepts that indicate that respect is actually a process of volitional judgment. By drawing upon Kant's transcendental idealism, however, the relationship between the two can be elucidated through the concept of the intelligible character, which serves as the ontological foundation of the empirical character. According to this interpretation, the mechanistic characterization of respect describes the empirical character, whereas the volitional characterization describes the intelligible character.[70]

Recall Kant's scale model in which pure practical reason removes the obstacles of inclination. There, Kant says that "*in the judgment of reason* this removal of a hindrance is *esteemed* equivalent to a positive furthering of its

---

[70] I thank the anonymous reviewer for pointing to this distinction.

causality" (5:75; emphasis mine). Likewise, Kant speaks of self-conceit not merely in terms of inclinations but in terms of "claims (*Ansprüche*) to esteem for oneself that precede accord with the moral law" (5:73). Normative attitudes toward the moral law, such as self-love and self-conceit are, according to the judgment model, propositional and volitional structures for which we bear responsibility.

According to the volitionalist account that I propose in this Element, inclinations and pure practical reason need to be interpreted from the perspective of an individual, self-reflective will. According to this account, the principle of sensibility and inclinations can be understood as the "propensity to make oneself, in accordance with the subjective determining grounds of one's power of choice, into an objective determining ground of the will in general," which can be called "self-conceit" (5:74). Self-conceit is neither a force that is opposed to pure practical reason as an object, nor a subject, and our will is thereby not properly described as a scale. Rather, self-conceit is a volitional and therefore imputable attitude toward the moral law. It is a propensity to make individual interests "the supreme practical condition," and thus must be excluded from the determination of the will. Referring to Kant's transcendental idealism, this can be understood in terms of a mechanistic opposition concerning the empirical character, and in terms of overweighing normative *moral reasons* by means of moral justification concerning the intelligible character.[71] As I shall argue next, we can better understand the justification model if we refer to Kant's conception of an "inner court" of conscience (6:438).

6.3 Disillusioning Self-Conceit

To outweigh self-conceit by moral reasons, we first need to understand how self-conceit works and how it is related to the capacity of practical reason. Moran (2014, 422) has pointed out the close proximity between the *attitude* of self-conceit and the *activity* of rationalizing. Generally speaking, self-conceit is about transgressing objective laws – it is, as Moran puts it, "the propensity to overstep or exceed (*übersteigen*) the boundaries of theoretical or practical reason" (2014, 423). In transgressing the moral law, self-conceit is closely related to Kant's notion of the dialectic of reason. In his *Critique of Pure Reason*, Kant speaks of the "logic of illusion," which he calls "a sophistical art for giving to its ignorance, indeed even to its intentional tricks, the air of truth, by imitating the method of thoroughness, which logic prescribes in

---

[71] See Reath 1989, 296. However, Herrera (2000, 400) has criticized Reath's intellectualism for assuming that moral acknowledgment by justification immediately leads to an action. Instead, he argues that "motives or reasons become operative only when accompanied by affective *Triebfedern*" (2000, 397).

general, and using its topics for the embellishment of every empty pretension" (B 86). Kant describes this active production of an "air of truth," which can be traced back to the individual use of reason, by virtue of the concept of "rationalizing" (*Vernünfteln*).[72]

From a practical point of view, self-conceit pertains to the subject's propensity to subordinate the universality of the moral law to individual interest. On closer inspection, self-conceit is not an external obstacle to practical reason, as the conflict and the scale model suggest but, as it involves rationalizing, an immoral *use* of reason. Focusing on the volitional activity of rationalizing, therefore, allows us to better understand the relationship between moral respect and self-conceit, and to understand Kant's thesis that respect "strikes down" self-conceit without referring to the conflict model in terms of separate forces or subjects. According to the volitionalist account, the autonomous will as a causality of reason captures crucial aspects of the conflict model, because it causally *restricts* the demands of sensibility, whereas the autonomous will as volitional self-consciousness and volitional judgment captures crucial aspects of the scale model, because the moral subject *evaluates* the moral law higher than the demands of sensibility.

In the *Groundwork*, Kant, using the scale model, speaks of a "powerful counterweight to all the commands of duty," which man "feels" in himself. Practical reason, by its universal and categorical commandment, restricts our individual needs, and from this a "natural dialectic" arises, which Kant defines as a "propensity to rationalize against those strict laws of duty" (4:405). The activity of this propensity consists in the attempt to argue, by means of reason, against the demand of the moral law, that is, to abuse reason.[73] As previously described, those who rationalize search for reasons to justify their individual interests as being exempt from the demand of the moral law, that is, "to cast doubt upon their validity, or at least upon their purity and strictness, and, where possible, to make them better suited to our wishes and inclinations, that is, to corrupt them" (4:407).

What is crucial about moral respect is that it is not just a feeling, but that it has a propositional structure manifesting itself in our own judgment and in our moral self-consciousness. This rational structure of respect becomes clear when Kant argues that in feeling respect, the human being "*compares* with it the

---

[72] For the concept of rationalizing in Kant, see Sticker (2021), Noller (2021), and Noller (2022). Papish (2018, 51) has interpreted the roots of rationalizing as our propensity to overdetermine our maxims.

[73] Sticker (2021, 3) has pointed out that rationality "enables us to seemingly justify moral transgressions to ourselves and others, and it creates an interest in such justifications in the first place." However, reason only enables us to rationalize if we *use* it in a rationalizing way.

sensible propensity of his nature" (5:74). This self-affirmation can be distinguished in a twofold *judgment*. On the one hand, compared to self-conceit, the moral law causes a state of humiliation and intellectual contempt (5:75). From the perspective of the judgment model, Kant's claim that the moral law "strikes down self-conceit altogether" can be understood in terms of recognizing "all claims to esteem for oneself that precede accord with the moral law" as "quite unwarranted" (5:73). This means that we recognize that the reasons that we give in the case of self-conceit are actually not moral reasons and therefore should not be motivating reasons, although they often are.

So far, however, moral respect manifests in terms of negative volitional self-recognition, which Kant describes as "pain" (5:73). Understanding pain in terms of the judgment and justification model, it is not properly understood in terms of harm or destruction but rather as disillusionment, a "lowering of pretensions to moral self-esteem" (5:79). Kant therefore describes pain in terms of "humiliation" and "intellectual contempt" (5:75), which is quite the opposite of respect, as can be seen in the German terms "Achtung" (*respect*) and "Verachtung" (*contempt*). Whoever is disillusioned is disappointed, and here we can see that the negative feeling of pain manifests itself in a negative attitude toward oneself, as a kind of negative self-consciousness.

6.4 Choice about Respect

We can understand moral respect in terms of a judgment that is not merely theoretical, but rather practical insofar it is based on a volitional comparison: "[T]he moral law unavoidably humiliates every human being when he *compares* with it the sensible propensity of his nature" (5:74; emphasis mine). This shows that the function of respect in moral motivation is not conceived of as a conflict of a subject's internal forces but of normatively conflicting propensities, understood as volitional structures, within an objective moral judgment. Respect is therefore not a conflict *before* the eyes of a moral subject but an argumentative dispute *in its very own will*. Whereas conscience is similar to moral respect in that it is "the moral faculty of judgment, passing judgment upon itself" (6:186), it does not, by judging, directly motivate us to act, as respect does according to the volitionalist account. However, through the self-evaluative function of conscience, it *indirectly* contributes to the process of moral motivation.[74] In his *Metaphysics of Morals*, Kant argues that conscience "is not directed to an object but merely to the subject (to affect moral feeling by its act)" (6:400). Although conscience mainly implies a *retrospective* concerning past actions, which has no direct motivational function, and which Kant

---

[74] I thank the reviewer for drawing my attention to this point.

describes as a "prosecutor" within a human agent, which "is the ground of repentance for a deed long past at every recollection of it" (5:98), consciousness also has a prospective (warning) function (6:440), insofar as it "speaks *long beforehand*," and even a simultaneous perspective on actions (27:43).

In his second *Critique*, Kant speaks of a "judgment of reason" (5:75; 5:76) that is directed to the moral law in feeling respect so that respect is to be understood as "morality itself subjectively considered as an incentive" (5:76). Likewise, Kant speaks of respect in terms of a "regard which the human being in his appraisals has for the moral law" (5:81). With regard to the judgment model of moral respect, there is a systematic connection to Kant's conception of moral consciousness as an "internal judge" (6:438). Even if moral respect is not identical to moral consciousness, because respect concerns the moral law, motives, and moral motivation, whereas moral conscience concerns moral actions, Kant's metaphor of an "*internal court*" can help us to better understand the justification model of the impact of respect. Kant argues that we must not conceive of the morally accused and the morally judging as identical. There needs to be another person, which Kant calls an "ideal person," "since the court is set up *within* man" (6:439). By applying the metaphor of an internal court to the phenomenon of moral respect, we can understand the objectivity of the moral law in terms of a volitional judgment that is compelling, thereby becoming a normative reason for action.

In his *Lectures on Ethics*, Kant distinguishes between the *arbitrium brutum* and *arbitrium liberum* (29:896). Whereas the former is determined or even necessitated by *stimuli* that concern our sensibility, the latter is determined by *motives*. Kant claims that a human being can indeed be affected by stimuli but not be *necessitated* by motives. If we apply this distinction to the judgment model of moral motivation, we see that it is about motives and not about stimuli. We can understand these motives in terms of normative reasons in order to avoid any reference to the conflict model and even the scale model, which understands moral motivation and moral choice in mechanical terms.[75] According to the volitionalist reading of moral respect, immoral reasons can be explained without referring to a cognitive error, as intellectualists do, and without understanding it in terms of empirical forces that overweigh rational forces. Rather, immoral reasons are due to a misuse of practical reason by rationalizing. Indeed, they imply a cognitive practical error that is imputable.

However, this still leaves the question open whether we ultimately act from respect for the moral law or from self-conceit: how can we be responsible for

---

[75] Schadow (2013, 50) distinguishes between normative and motivational reasons regarding the moral feeling of respect. However, she does not discuss these reasons regarding the question of determinism and electivism about moral respect.

judging in such a way that we prefer self-conceit over respect for the moral law and follow our judgment with an action? I shall discuss this question in Section 8, when it comes to the duty of cultivating respect and moral feelings in order for them to finally become motivating reasons. I shall argue that we need to interpret electivism about moral respect in terms of cultivism, which makes the imputability of our moral choice even more apparent.

7 Feeling Reason: The Phenomenology of Moral Respect

In this section, I shall mainly discuss Kant's Emotion Thesis about moral respect, thereby referring to Kant's third *Critique* and his "system of our cognitive faculties" (20:244). As we have seen in the previous section, Kant understands the impact of respect as enabling the transition from mere legality to morality by an intentionality that can be described as moral self-consciousness and self-recognition. What is important about this transition is that it needs to be a subjective state in which the moral subject is causally directly related to the moral law. This causal relationship to the moral law, since it is subjective, needs to be explained not only from a systematic perspective of pure practical reason but also from a volitional first-person perspective to realize the transition from legality to morality. Such a phenomenology of respect is best understood in terms of a volitionalist account, since, as I have shown earlier, the human will as a twofold determinable human faculty allows mediating between reason and sensibility.[76]

7.1 Feeling Respect

As we have seen in the previous section, Kant uses aesthetic terminology in his chapter on the incentives of pure practical reason, referring to feeling but also the moral sublime. Accordingly, I will link these descriptions to Kant's third *Critique* and discuss the relationship of the faculty of desire as practical reason with the power of judgment as the faculty of feeling of pleasure and displeasure. Discussing the power of judgment to analyze Kant's notion of respect is justified given my endorsement of the volitional judgment model over the conflict and scale model of moral motivation. Kant himself connects all three human faculties with regard to the problem of freedom:

> it is surely enough to produce a connection *a priori* between the feeling of pleasure and the other two faculties if we connect a cognition *a priori*, namely the rational concept of freedom, with the faculty of desire as its determining

---

[76] For a phenomenological approach to Kant's concept of respect, without referring to a volitionalist account, see Drummond (2006), Lipscomb (2010), Kriegel/Timmons (2021).

ground, at the same time subjectively finding in this objective determination a feeling of pleasure contained in the determination of the will. (20:206–7)

However, Kant notes that the moral feeling of respect takes a special role:

> To establish *a priori* the connection of the feeling of a pleasure or displeasure as an effect with some representation (sensation or concept) as its cause is absolutely impossible, for that would be a causal relation, which (among objects of experience) can only ever be cognized *a posteriori* and by means of experience itself. To be sure, in the critique of practical reason we actually derived the feeling of respect (as a special and peculiar modification of this feeling, which will not coincide exactly either with the pleasure or with the displeasure that we obtain from empirical objects) from universal moral concepts *a priori*. (5:221–2)

Kant goes on, arguing that "there we could also step beyond the bounds of experience and appeal to a causality that rests on a supersensible property of the subject, namely that of freedom." Yet, according to Kant's epistemology, it is not possible to *positively* cognize how reason can directly determine the will. In his third *Critique*, Kant argues that we

> cannot expect to determine a priori the influence that a given representation has on the mind, as we previously noticed in the Critique of Practical Reason, where the representation of a universal lawfulness of willing must at one and the same time determine the will and thereby also arouse the feeling of respect, as a law contained, and indeed contained a priori, in our moral judgments, even though this feeling could nonetheless not be derived from concepts. (20:239)

From this quotation it becomes clear that the judgment model of moral motivation can explain how the feeling of respect motivates us, whereas intellectualism cannot, since, as Kant argues, the moral feeling of respect cannot be derived from theoretical concepts but only from "universal moral concepts *a priori*" (5:222), which supports the volitionalist account.

Due to the epistemological restrictions of transcendental idealism, Kant argues that we cannot "show a priori ... the ground from which the moral law in itself supplies an incentive," because "how a law can be of itself and immediately a determining ground of the will ... is for human reason an insoluble problem and identical with that of how a free will is possible." Rather, we can show a priori "what it effects (or, to put it better, must effect) in the mind insofar as it is an incentive" (5:72). Hence, we need to analyze respect in terms of "the phenomenal etiology of morally worthy action" (Guyer 2016, 236), which Ware (2014, 734) has discussed by distinguishing between a third-person perspective that concerns "the question of reason's causal efficacy," and a first-person perspective, which concerns "the question of what the moral law must feel like." Similarly, Lipscomb (2010, 61–2) has argued that due to epistemological restrictions, Kant explains the effects of the moral law on sensibility in terms of a "phenomenological narrative" in order to give at least an *indirect* account of the formation of rational moral motivation, that is, "to determine carefully in what way the moral law becomes the incentive and, inasmuch as it is, what happens to the human faculty of desire as an effect of that determining ground upon it" (5:72). From this quotation we can see that the phenomenology of respect is deeply linked to Kant's complex notion of the will. I shall argue that Kant's phenomenology of the moral feeling of respect must be understood from a volitional perspective.

The will insofar as it can be determined by the moral law allows understanding moral respect from both a systematic and a phenomenological perspective. We can *understand* autonomy from the perspective of a causality of reason, and we can *feel* autonomy from the first-person perspective. Referring to Kant's notion of the will allows us to understand respect both in terms of a feeling, as affectivists do, and as an intelligible cause and judgment, as intellectualists do (see Section 4.4). Admittedly, "[a]ffectivists need not deny that Kantian moral motivation initially arises from an intellectual recognition of the moral law," as McCarty (1993, 423) has put it. However, affectivism leaves the question open of how exactly moral feeling and intellectual recognition of the moral law are related, not to mention their *normative* relationship. Opposed to affectivism and intellectualism, the volitionalist account holds that the moral feeling of respect can be explained by referring to the self-reflective process of moral autonomy. As such, respect has both an intellectual and affective dimension that are mediated by the moral will. Therefore, according to the volitionalist account, the human will can be understood from the perspective of objective rational and moral determination by the moral law (the ideal third-person perspective of a causality of reason) and from the first-person perspective of the agent's own point of view, which manifests in terms of a feeling. Moral respect demands these two perspectives, since they cover the objectivity and normativity of the moral law and the subjectivity of being morally motivated.

Attempting to unify both perspectives, Guevara (2000, 100) has argued that the moral feeling of respect is "the embodiment of the law." I agree with this interpretation, since, as we have seen earlier, respect is deeply linked with "the system of our cognitive faculties" (20:244) – that is, reason, will, and the power of judgment. What I want to stress, however, is the central notion of the self-reflective will in terms of autonomy for this embodiment or expression of the moral law, since it allows mediating between reason and sensibility.

As we have seen in the previous section, the judgment model has many advantages over the conflict and the scale model of moral motivation. In this section, I shall interpret the moral feeling of respect from the perspective of the capacity to judge, which Kant in his third *Critique* understands in terms of the "[f]eeling of pleasure and displeasure" (5:198). In doing so, I focus on Kant's use of the concepts of sublimity and elevation, which he refers to frequently in his second *Critique* (5:87–8).

It is obvious that the double-sidedness of the moral feeling of respect – its unity of submission and elevation – reveals a close connection to the phenomenon of the dynamic sublime in Kant's *Critique of the Power of Judgement*, but also contains crucial differences. Focusing on Kant's theory of the sublime in the third *Critique* from the perspective of the power of judgment helps to better understand Kant's Emotion Thesis about respect. I shall argue that there is a structural analogy between the feeling of respect and the feeling of the sublime in terms of the power of judgment. The difference, however, is that the feeling of respect must also be understood in terms of our faculty of desire, whereas the feeling of the sublime may not, since it is volitionally and normatively indifferent and therefore not eligible for strict moral motivation.[77] This does not rule out the possibility and even duty to integrate the feeling of the sublime into a kind of moral pedagogy, as I shall explain in Section 8.

Kant discusses the phenomenon of moral respect with regard to the phenomenon of the (dynamic) sublime, thereby referring to the power of judgment. From the perspective of the sublime, Kant defines respect negatively as "[t]he feeling of the inadequacy of our capacity for the attainment of an idea." He argues that in feeling, the sublime must be understood in terms of a twofold *judgment*. As "a feeling of displeasure," it results "from the inadequacy of the imagination in the aesthetic estimation of magnitude for the estimation by means of reason." As a feeling of "pleasure," it is "aroused at the same time from the correspondence of this very judgment of the inadequacy of the greatest sensible faculty in comparison with ideas of reason." Therefore, "whatever arouses the feeling of this supersensible vocation in us is in agreement with that law" (5:257). The feeling of the dynamic sublime is a kind of moral self-recognition in our judgment about nature. However, it "is not contained in anything in nature, but only in our mind, insofar as we can become conscious of being superior to nature within us and thus also to nature outside us" (5:264).

However, the moral self-recognition of the feeling of the sublime is not volitional and therefore cannot be understood in terms of moral autonomy.

---

[77] In line with my argument, Merritt (2018, 59) has argued that "the non-exhortative character of admiration shows it to be a more suitable candidate for the feeling for natural sublimity than respect."

Kant emphasizes that the feeling of the aesthetic sublime is only analogous to the moral feeling of respect. The feeling of the sublime "is *represented* only as a power of the mind to soar above certain obstacles of sensibility by means of moral principles, and thereby to become interesting" (5:271; my emphasis). Although there are many similarities between the aesthetic and the moral phenomenon of the sublime, there is a decisive difference.[78] The dynamic sublime is projected into nature, whereas in the case of moral respect it is not a metaphorical transfer but a real and actual normative relation. From this follows that the moral sublime has a motivating power, whereas the aesthetic sublime is not a volitional attitude. The reason for the dynamic sublime being motivationally inert is that it is not directly connected to the moral law as the moral sublime is. The moral sublime, however, can be understood and felt in terms of moral autonomy. Kant therefore argues that "[t]he majesty of the law ... instills awe (not dread, which repels; and also not fascination, which invites familiarity); and this awe rouses the respect of the subject toward his master, except that in this case, since the master lies in us, it rouses a *feeling of the sublimity* of our own vocation that enraptures us more than any beauty" (6:23 n.). From this passage follows that the phenomenon of the aesthetic sublime is a merely derived form of the moral sublime that lacks its volitional dimension.

Kant stresses the priority of the moral over the aesthetic, which consists in another kind of *interest*. Whereas "[t]he beautiful pleases immediately (but only in reflecting intuition, not, like morality, in the concept)" and "without any interest," "the morally good is of course necessarily connected with an interest, but not with one that precedes the judgment on the satisfaction, but rather with one that is thereby first produced" (5:354). The moral interest in feeling respect is causally grounded in the moral law and in its volitional reflection and judgment, whereas the aesthetic feeling is not.

7.2 Moral and Aesthetic Sublimity

The reason for the normative difference between the moral and the aesthetic phenomenon of the sublime consists in the fact that, in case of morality, the power that humiliates the sensible subject and the power that elevates the moral subject are judged as *identical*. Yet, in the case of the aesthetic sublime, it is the force of nature which overwhelms the subject's sensible side. It is actually reason that elevates the moral subject:

> [T]he feeling of the sublime in nature is respect for our own vocation, which we show to an object in nature through a certain subreption (substitution of

---

[78] These differences have been noted, among others, by Beck (1960, 220), McCarty (1993, 434), and Merritt (2018, 59–60).

> a respect for the object instead of for the idea of humanity in our subject), which as it were makes intuitable the superiority of the rational vocation of our cognitive faculty over the greatest faculty of sensibility. (5:257)

The phenomenon of moral respect, however, does not consist in some kind of experience of nature but of one's own internal moral nature that produces a feeling of freedom that Kant identifies with a sort of "contentment with oneself," because of the moral subject's higher vocation, which consists in its self-reflective volitional "independence from the inclinations" (5:117). Here we can see that, due to a subreption, the feeling of the sublime in nature is not an expression of autonomy, whereas the moral feeling of respect is.

The moral feeling of respect, as Kant describes it, is not a simple, heteronomous feeling, but consists in a process of volitional self-determination. Moral respect reflects the different stances an individual subject can take toward the moral law, according to its complex intentionality as discussed in Section 5. In the course of the process of moral self-consciousness, the subject passes through three different volitional stages and emotional attitudes toward the moral law, which can be linked to the process of volitional moral autonomy discussed earlier. To be sure, these stages are not to be understood in terms of temporal events, as part of a developmental process over time, but are rather three aspects of the phenomenology of respect.

The negative effect upon feeling, which Kant describes as a sort of disagreeableness, "is *pathological*, as is every influence on feeling and every feeling in general" (5:75). At this stage, the moral subject is not yet able to appreciate the absolute worth of morality. It is still indifferent toward normativity and thus experiences the moral law merely as an *external* force that painfully restricts self-conceit. In a second step, the moral subject gains legal consciousness as it recognizes the feeling of pain "[a]s the effect of consciousness of the moral law" (5:75). The result of this confrontation of pain "in relation to an intelligible cause … namely the subject of pure practical reason as the supreme lawgiver" (5:75) is what Kant calls the attitude of "humiliation" and "intellectual contempt" (5:75), as the moral subject recognizes its propensity to make its individual interests become an objective determining ground of the will. At this state of consciousness, however, the moral law is still conceived of as something external that is different and separated from the subject's own existence, which is not sufficient for morality. In a third and final step, the subject recognizes "its positive ground" (5:75), which is distinguished from its individual and empirical nature, as it is the universal moral law itself as expressed in humanity. As such, moral respect appears as moral self-respect, which is an expression of moral autonomy.

Kant differentiates between various kinds of judgments. With regard to aesthetic reflective judgments, he distinguishes the agreeable, the beautiful, the sublime, and the absolutely, that is, morally good (5:266). Whereas the agreeable depends merely on quantity, the beautiful depends on quality. The sublime concerns nature as being "judged as suitable for a possible supersensible use of it" (5:267), so that it is structurally analogous to the absolutely good "as the determinability of the powers of the subject by means of the representation of an *absolutely necessitating* law." However, from a modal perspective, a judgment about the morally good is not merely a claim about facts but a normative command about what *should* be the case. Therefore, it is not an "aesthetic" but an "intellectual power of judgment." Since it does not concern nature but freedom, it is not merely a reflecting but a *determining* judgment (5:267). Whereas a reflecting judgment cannot determine our will in terms of normative reasons, a determining judgment can.

However, the fact that aesthetic sublimity does not motivate moral actions in terms of normative reasons does not mean that it plays no role for moral motivation. Rather, Kant argues that it needs to be cultivated, because the moral feeling of respect "is nevertheless related to the aesthetic power of judgment and its *formal conditions* to the extent that it can serve to make the lawfulness of action out of duty representable at the same time as aesthetic, i.e., as sublime, or also as beautiful, without sacrificing any of its purity" (5:267). In the next section, I shall argue that similarly to the feeling of the sublime, the moral feeling of respect is subject to cultivation. For in his second *Critique*, Kant argues that "[i]t is something very sublime in human nature to be determined to actions directly by a pure rational law, and even the illusion that takes the subjective side of this intellectual determinability of the will as something aesthetic" (5:117).

8 Cultivating Morality: The Education of Respect

In this section, I discuss how Kant conceives of the cultivation of respect, and how this cultivation allows combining the moral feeling of respect with related feelings such as love and compassion. In doing so, I will especially address Kant's Normativity Thesis, according to which (i) we have the duty to cultivate the moral feeling of respect, (ii) the moral feeling of respect is the basis (*Grund*) for duties, and (iii) we have the duty to show respect to other persons, both in moral and epistemological regards.

Respect, as an expression of moral self-consciousness and autonomy, is a feeling that needs to be cultivated. Kant argues that reason needs "to work itself up so as to gather strength to resist the inclinations by a lively representation of the dignity of the law" (5:147). Therefore, Kant demands us "to cultivate as much as possible the effect of reason on this feeling" (5:118). We can understand the duty of cultivating the moral feeling of respect in terms of cultivating moral autonomy. To be sure, since the moral law causes the moral feeling of respect, there can be no duty to feel respect as such. However, we are responsible for *how* we cultivate the moral feeling of respect in such a way that in feeling respect, we intentionally direct and coordinate all our faculties of the mind to the moral law to respect ourselves and other persons.

8.1 Cultivating Respect

According to cultivism about moral respect, we are subject to the duty of moral cultivation. Therefore, we are responsible for developing moral self-consciousness such that we can avoid self-conceit, since we are also able to fall prey to the illusion of self-conceit by means of rationalizing, as I have argued in Section 6. This educational role of the moral feeling of respect has been highlighted by several authors.[79] In this section, I shall situate Kant's educational discussion about respect in the larger context of Kant's statements about respect, especially with regard to his Singularity Thesis, his Intentionality Thesis, and his Normativity Thesis. I shall argue that the moral feeling of respect is of crucial importance for moral education since it allows cultivating autonomy and allows a subject to develop moral responsibility, although we do not have the duty to *have* respect. This speaks against a determinist conception of moral respect, according to which feeling respect is sufficient for an imputable action. Rather, it speaks for electivism about moral respect, because it depends on our cultivation and choice whether we act from moral respect and not from self-conceit.[80]

From a volitionalist perspective, the way we relate to the moral feeling of respect depends on us, so that we bear responsibility not only for whether we incorporate it into our maxim, as Kant argues in his *Religion* (6:27–8) and *Metaphysics of Morals* (6:226), but also whether and how we *cultivate* it. Indeed, we are, as Kant claims, "never able to lose the incentive that consists in the respect for the moral law" (6:46). This would render our moral imputability for good and evil actions impossible. In other words, we are not responsible for *having* the incentive of moral respect, which is necessary for moral imputability at all, but for cultivating its intentionality toward the moral law and our susceptibility for it. As such, it is up to us whether and how we realize the

---

[79] McCarty (1993, 421), Baxley (2010, 149), Herrera (2000, 407), Goy (2010, 169–74). For a discussion of the cultivation of feelings in general, see Cohen (2017).

[80] After Kant, Fichte would even argue that it is up to us how the moral law appears in our consciousness and that we are responsible for obscuring its representation. See Noller (2023).

transition from mere legality to morality. Since the transition from legality to morality describes the Kantian notion of autonomy as moral self-consciousness and self-respect, the cultivation of moral respect essentially is a cultivation of moral autonomy.

If we can and indeed should cultivate our moral feeling of respect, it follows that we have to behave toward it such that it is subject to our choice. According to Kant's Normativity Thesis, we are not responsible for feeling respect *at all* but for maintaining our susceptibility for it. We have, as Kant puts it, "a *susceptibility* on the part of free choice to be moved by pure practical reason (and its law), and this is what we call moral feeling" (6:400). Since, as Kant argues in his *Religion* (6:45), "ought" implies "can," we are not responsible for having incentives but for cultivating them, and for how we incorporate them into our maxims (6:45 n.). In what follows, I shall call this Kant's educational account of respect. This account is not based on the third or first-person perspective, but on a genetical and educational perspective by means of concrete examples in the double sense of the word – by concrete situations and by exemplary models of moral behavior. Therefore, the educational account of moral respect entails both a first-person and second-person perspective: We are responsible for cultivating our own moral feelings, and we are, as parents and teachers, responsible for the moral education and cultivation of our children's moral feelings.

According to the educational account of respect, from a first-person perspective moral education does not concern concrete moral behavior in terms of actions. Rather, it concerns our maxims and, as such, "the transformation" of our moral "character" (6:48). In his *Religion*, Kant stresses the importance of the "feeling of the sublimity of our moral vocation," because it helps "awakening moral dispositions, since it directly counters the innate propensity to pervert the incentives in the maxims of our power of choice" (6:50). Feeling the moral sublime implies that we feel and judge our propensity for self-conceit inferior to our moral nature.

In his second *Critique*, Kant understands the doctrine of methods of pure practical reason as "the method of founding and cultivating genuine moral dispositions" (5:153), which concerns the transition from legality to morality. Referring to the original sense of the Greek word *méthodos*, he understands it as "the way in which one can provide the laws of pure practical reason with *access* to the human mind and *influence* on its maxims, that is, the way in which one can make objectively practical reason *subjectively* practical as well" (5:141). Kant's method of moral education aims to sensitize our "receptivity to a pure moral interest" (5:152), which can be understood in terms of our susceptibility for the moral feeling of respect. Thereby, he analyzes the phenomenology of respect in terms of a genetic and educational account. However, according to Kant, the doctrine of method "is only preparatory" and merely intended as "outlines" (5:161). In his subsequent *Metaphysics of Morals*, Kant discusses the moral education of respect at greater length.

From a second-person perspective, the cultivation of respect concerns the moral education of children. Interestingly, the subject of moral education in Kant's example is not an abstract finite rational being, as he is mainly referring to in various places of his second *Critique*,[81] but "a ten-year-old boy" (5:155). In his *Religion*, Kant claims that "even children are capable of discovering even the slightest taint of admixture of spurious incentives." To cultivate the "predisposition to the good" of children, understood as "apprentices in morality," we need to proceed in two steps. First, we need to provide "the *example* of good people (as regards their conformity to law)." This first stage concerns the legality of actions but not the morality of dispositions. Therefore, the second stage of morality demands "to judge the impurity of certain maxims on the basis of the incentives actually behind their actions." Thereby, "the predisposition gradually becomes an attitude of mind, so that *duty* merely for itself begins to acquire in the apprentice's heart a noticeable importance" (6:48).

Similarly, in Kant's second *Critique*, the way of moral education and pedagogy consists in presenting morally distinguished examples by means of moral narratives of a person that refuses to defame another innocent person. This moral refusal is increasingly challenged by (i) temptations of reward, (ii) threat of loss of wealth and life, and (iii) arousal of greatest fear and painful compassion with her closest relatives. Like in his *Religion*, the method of moral education proceeds "step by step." At the same time, Kant here conceives of moral education as a process containing three steps "from (i) mere approval to (ii) admiration, from that to amazement, and finally (iii) to the greatest veneration" (5:156; my annotations). Moral self-consciousness cannot be realized immediately "by inspiring enthusiasm" to children, which "is tantamount to soon making them fantasizers" (5:157). Rather, moral education needs to follow a method, beginning with mere (legal) approval and leading into (moral) respect. According to Kant, "this exercise and the consciousness of a cultivation of our reason in judging merely about the practical, arising from this exercise, must gradually produce a certain interest in reasons's law itself and hence in morally good actions" (5:159–60).

With that in mind, Kant stresses that "this employment of the faculty of judgment, which lets us feel our own cognitive powers, is not yet interest in actions and in their morality itself" (5:160). Therefore, we need a "*second* exercise," which

---

[81] See for example 5:25; 5:27; 5:33; 5:34; 5:79; 5:80; 5:82; 5:86; 5:101; 5:111; 5:123.

does not concern the legality of actions but concerns "the moral disposition in examples." Since the moral feeling of respect is not yet fully developed, Kant addresses the Freedom Thesis and the Emotion Thesis. By focusing on "the purity of will," the moral subject feels freedom in the negative sense in terms of "pain" insofar as the volitional purity is first judged in terms of "renunciation." However, from the perspective of positive freedom, the moral subject's "mind is made receptive to the feeling of satisfaction from other sources" (5:161). Kant argues that by the second exercise, which concerns morality, "the law of duty, through the positive worth that observance of it lets us feel, finds easier access through the *respect for ourselves* in the consciousness of our freedom" (5:161). What is important here is that moral respect is not *sufficient* for moral action but only *supports* it. As I have argued in Section 2.3, respect does not lead to a moral action without choice. Whereas the moral feeling of respect determines the will, it does not determine our faculty of choice. Therefore, we are responsible for incorporating moral respect into our maxim.

8.2 The Duty of Respect

In his *Metaphysics of Morals*, Kant formulates his Normativity Thesis, claiming that a person "must have respect for the law within himself in order even to think of any duty whatsoever" (6:403). To justify his Normativity Thesis, Kant argues by means of a reductio ad absurdum (6:402–3):

(1) We have the duty of respect toward ourselves.
(2) Having the duty of respect toward ourselves presupposes to "be presented to us only through the *respect* we have for it."
(3) "A duty to have respect would thus amount to being put under obligation to [have] duties," which is a contradiction.
(4) "Accordingly it is not correct to say that a man has a *duty of self-esteem;* it must rather be said that the law within him unavoidably forces from him *respect* for his own being,"
(5) The moral feeling of respect "is the basis (*Grund*) of certain duties, that is, of certain actions that are consistent with his duty to himself."
(6) "It cannot be said that a man *has* a duty of respect toward himself, for he must have respect for the law within himself in order even to think of any duty whatsoever."

Given that moral respect is the susceptibility for duties, as Kant argues (6:400), it cannot be a duty itself. Rather, respect is the very condition of having and recognizing duties, because "any consciousness of obligation depends upon moral feeling to make us aware of the constraint present in the thought of duty"

(6:399). Kant emphasizes that "there can be no duty to have moral feeling or to acquire it; instead every man (as a moral being) has it in him originally" (6:399). In addition, although every finite rational being has the propensity of moral respect toward the moral law, as well as the susceptibility for moral respect (6:27), we have the duty "to *cultivate* it and to strengthen it through wonder at its inscrutable source" (6:399), because we are also subject to our propensity for evil.

Yet how exactly can we cultivate the moral feeling of respect? Drawing on Section 8.1, I will be showing in what follows that the cultivation of respect requires (i) being conscious of and training one's capacity to overweigh the principle of natural inclinations as expressed by self-conceit and self-love, which also implies conscience, and (ii) being careful about being contemptuous of other people – be it in practical or theoretical regards. I shall call the former the duty of the cultivation of our volitional moral self-consciousness[82] and conscience,[83] and the latter the duty to respect the other's practical and epistemic *dignity*. To be sure, Kant understands conscience as "the capacity to become conscious of the rightfulness or wrongfulness of all of one's actions" (18:579) and insofar as a kind of moral self-consciousness. However, conscience is not consciousness of moral actions *as such* but the reflective awareness of an "examination of actions (whether they are right or wrong)" so that in conscience "reason judges itself," since "it is understanding, not conscience, which judges whether an action is in general right or wrong" (6:186).

Kant argues that "[e]very man has a legitimate claim to respect from his fellow men and is *in turn* (*wechselseitig*) bound to respect every other" (6:463). Respect is therefore a twofold relation that holds mutually between persons, and persons toward themselves. Respecting other people means to avoid using a person "merely as a means," that is as a "thing," but rather that a person must "always be used at the same time as an end." From a second-person perspective, this means that every person has "a duty regarding the respect that must be shown to every other man" (6:462).

Directly opposed to respect for others is what Kant calls "[t]o be *contemptuous* of others (*contemnere*), that is, to deny them the respect owed to men in general" (6:464). Being shown respect does not depend on moral behavior, because "even a vicious man as a man" deserves respect, "in his quality as a man, even though by his deeds he makes himself unworthy of it" (6:464). By respecting an immorally acting person we ensure that this person is able to respect herself after all and does not lose, as being socially condemned, her very

---

[82] For the duty of self-knowledge and its relationship to moral respect, see Ware (2019, 680).
[83] In his *Metaphysics of Morals*, Kant argues that it is our duty "to cultivate one's conscience, to sharpen one's attentiveness to the voice of the inner judge, and to use every means to obtain a hearing for it" (6:401).

self-respect. Therefore, "showing respect for man as a moral being (holding his duty in highest esteem) is also a duty that others have toward him and a right to which he cannot renounce his claim" (6:464).

According to Kant, we not only have the duty to respect a person from a practical point of view but also from an epistemic point of view, which Kant calls the "duty to respect a man even in the logical use of his reason" (6:463). Epistemic respect does not concern our intentionality and judgment toward the moral law but to truth, that is, another person's *epistemic dignity* understood as "respect for his own understanding." Our epistemic duty toward another person's epistemic dignity demands "not to censure his errors by calling them absurdities, poor judgment and so forth." Rather, showing another person's epistemic dignity respect means "to suppose that his judgment must yet contain some truth," from which follows our epistemic duty as to "uncovering ... the deceptive illusion (the subjective ground that determined his judgment that, by an oversight, he took for objective), and so, by explaining to him the possibility of his having erred, to preserve his respect for his own understanding" (6:463). Kant argues that "[t]he same thing applies to the censure of vice, which must never break out into complete contempt and denial of any moral worth to a vicious man; for on this supposition he could never be improved, and this is not consistent with the Idea of a *man,* who as such (as a moral being) can never lose entirely his predisposition to the good" (6:644–5). Kant calls the "failure to fulfill the duty arising from the *respect* owed to every man as such ... a *vice (vitium).*" Generally, a vice is something that "abolishes the worth of what would otherwise be to the subject's good" (6:464).

The duty of virtue demands self-knowledge and self-mastery, that is, "cultivating one's capacities" as a kind of personal formation, which finally amounts to the "duty to carry the cultivation of his *will* up to the purest virtuous disposition, in which the *law* becomes also the incentive to his actions" (6:387). This means that the moral law must not only be a normative reason but also a motivating reason. The cultivation of the will in terms of virtue leads to what Kant calls the "autocracy of reason," which applies to finite human beings and "involves consciousness of the capacity to master one's inclinations when they rebel against the law" (6:383). In his *Lectures on Ethics*, Kant argues that "[m]astery over ourselves is also more difficult because the moral law has precepts, indeed, but no motives; it lacks executive authority, and this is the moral feeling." "[S]elf-mastery," as Kant puts it, "rests on the strength of the moral feeling" (27:361). Indeed, Kant here uses the conflict model of moral motivation. However, according to cultivism about respect, we are responsible for whether and how we cultivate our will and how our autocracy comes to moral consciousness. Kant characterizes the relationship between conscience, respect, and autocracy as follows:

> He who would discipline himself morally must pay great attention to himself, and often give an account of his actions before the inner judge, since then, by long practice, he will have given strength to the moral motivating grounds, and acquired, by cultivation, a habit of desire or aversion in regard to moral good or evil. By this the moral feeling will be cultivated, and then morality will have strength and motivation; by these motives, sensibility will be weakened and overcome, and in this way self-command will be achieved. (27:361)

8.3 Respect, Love, and Friendship

From the perspective of cultivation and virtue, Kant reconsiders the relationship between respect and love. Whereas Kant, according to his Singularity Thesis, had argued that respect is "the sole and also the undoubted moral incentive,"[84] he now considers moral respect and love as a complementary relationship. Kant illustrates the complementarity of respect and love as part of his conception of friendship as "the union of two persons through equal mutual love and respect" (6:469). He claims that this emotional state is only an "ideal" and "unattainable in practice" but nevertheless "a duty set by reason" (6:469). Since friendship is a duty, we are morally responsible for cultivating and establishing such a relationship, and thereby the moral feeling of respect plays a major role.

To explain the constitution of friendship, Kant refers to the phenomenology of love and respect as "great moral forces." In terms of attraction, "[t]he principle of mutual love admonishes men constantly to *come closer* to one another." In terms of repulsion, "the respect they owe one another" causes the members of friendship "to keep themselves *at a distance* from one another" (6:449). In the same way that we can avoid a "conflict-of-forces conception of agency" (Allison 1990, 126) from a volitionalist point of view when it comes to duty and inclination (see Section 6.1), we can avoid a "unity-of-forces conception of agency" when it comes to love and respect. Love is an emotion that involves an attitude of judging the loving and the loved subject as being united. According to the "union view," "love consists in the formation of (or the desire to form) some significant kind of union, a 'we.',", which cancels out the differences (Helm 2021). Moral respect avoids that the distinction between two autonomous subjects is canceled out. However, it also prevents the two subjects from being in a relationship of mere moral indifference to one another.

From a volitionalist point of view, the emotion of respect involves an attitude of judging the other subject as being an end in itself, whose autonomy must not

---

[84] "Respect for the moral law is ... the sole and also the undoubted moral incentive" (5:78).

be restricted by coming too close. Hence, the distance involved in moral respect is not to be confused with disinterest or even hostility or fear.[85] Rather, it is an expression of esteeming the absolute dignity and autonomy of the other person, which can only be maintained from a point of view that is *distinct* from that of the other. This distance of respect is in line with Kant's Intentionality Thesis, according to which it is not primarily directed toward another person but to the moral law. Our relationship of respect toward another person needs to be grounded in the moral law, and this grounding relation distinguishes respect from love insofar as respect implies a distance toward another person, which must not be confused with ignorance but is rather a structural feature of *moral interest*. This moral interest, however, is not directed toward another person insofar as she is a subject with individual qualities but rather insofar as she is a subject of the moral law.

Yet, at a first glance, and opposed to his Singularity Thesis, Kant seems to argue that both respect and love are likewise necessary for morality, since "should one of these great moral forces fail ... then nothingness (immorality), with gaping throat, would drink up the whole kingdom of (moral) beings like a drop of water" (6:449). Likewise, Kant discusses mutual love and respect in terms of "virtues of social intercourse" (6:473). According to his account of friendship, it is a duty "not to *isolate* oneself ... but to use one's moral perfections in social intercourse." Whereas (self-)respect leads to "making oneself a fixed center of one's principles," this stage of autonomy needs to be extended to other persons by means of love. Kant argues for extending the moral center of respect as "forming part of an all-inclusive circle of those who, in their disposition, are citizens of the world" (6:473). This demands "to cultivate a disposition of reciprocity – agreeableness, tolerance, mutual love and respect," which, according to Kant, "is itself a duty of virtue" (6:473).

At a first glance, Kant's Singularity Thesis seems to be restricted when he says that we must not "avoid sharing painful feelings," as Kant argues, "[f]or this is still one of the impulses that nature has implanted in us to do what the representation of duty alone would not accomplish" (6:457). However, we can understand the coexistence and even duty to cultivate feelings like compassion and pity if we consider Kant's Normativity Thesis. Kant had argued that respect for the moral law is the "ground" of duties and that a person "must have respect for the law within himself in order even to think of any duty whatsoever" (6:403). The cultivation of moral respect is therefore a direct duty, whereas the cultivation of sympathy and similar feelings are just an indirect duty.[86]

---

[85] Baron (1997, 30), however, argues that it is "intuitively odd ... that respect bids us to hold back from others, while love bids us to approach them."

[86] See also Klemme (2006, 136n.), however not regarding the problem of moral imputability.

Kant's Singularity Thesis, according to which the moral feeling of respect is "the sole and also the undoubted moral incentive" (5:78), needs to be specified insofar as its singularity is not to be understood in terms of *exclusivity* but rather in terms of *priority*.

In line with the complementary function of respect, which does not contradict Kant's Singularity Thesis but rather specifies it, Kant argues that we have the duty to "establish" (*gründen*) and "cultivate" a feeling which he calls "satisfaction (*Zufriedenheit*) with oneself" (5:38) and "intellectual contentment" (5:118). This feeling arises when we determine our will according to the moral law in "frequent practice" (5:38), as a kind of second nature. It is, as Kant puts it, "an analogue of happiness that must necessarily accompany consciousness of virtue" (5:117).

9 Conclusion: Solving the Puzzle

Respect, as we have seen so far, is a complex phenomenon that addresses many levels of description and perspectives, with regard both to the human faculties of the mind and to moral phenomenology. Many problems and apparent mysteries of the puzzle of respect are due to a lack of differentiation between these faculties and perspectives. I have argued that we can make sense of Kant's rather enigmatic statements on the moral feeling of respect by considering its special volitional status within Kant's larger framework of rational autonomy, and by applying it to a complex model of human will and the faculties of the human mind.

The process of a will's moral formation is what Kant refers to as the formation of a causality of freedom, and which allows us to cultivate moral respect and to consider this cultivation a duty. As such, the moral feeling of respect marks the volitional center of moral motivation. Due to its complex intentionality, it concerns the transition from mere legality to morality. Thereby, it portrays the different human dispositions and stances toward the moral law, and demonstrates its unity at the same time. The moral feeling of respect is thus best understood as a free agent's volitional self-evaluation from a moral standpoint, both as a human animal *and* a rational human. Since all human faculties are concerned, the subject of respect *feels*, *wills*, *judges*, and *cognizes* morality. As such, moral respect is closely related to conscience, which Kant defines "as *the moral faculty of judgment, passing judgment upon itself*" (6:186). Thereby, conscience plays an important epistemic role for moral action. However, conscience is not directly connected to our faculty of the will, as moral respect is, although it is connected with moral respect. In his *Metaphysics of Morals*, Kant argues that "[e]very human being has a conscience and finds himself observed, threatened, and, in general, kept in awe (respect coupled with fear) by an internal judge" (6:438). In opposition to moral respect, this awe does not motivate us to act morally, but rather to refrain from immoral actions. Its motivating power is indirect, whereas that of moral respect is positive. However, through its judgment function, conscience can epistemically supplement respect and therefore has an indirect influence on our will for moral motivation.

On the basis of the complex structure of interacting human faculties, we can finally illuminate the seven characteristics that Kant attributed to the moral feeling of respect:

(i) Rationality Thesis: Respect is a volitional structure that has its causal determining ground in the moral law of pure practical reason and its reflection. It is only due to this rational origin that a moral agent acts autonomously and independently from natural inclinations. The moral law grounds the moral feeling of respect. Properly cultivated, the moral feeling allows us to withstand our propensity for self-conceit.

(ii) Singularity Thesis: Due to its rational basis and self-reflective structure, and due to its interconnectedness with the human faculties of understanding, desire, and the power of judgment, the moral feeling of respect allows for moral judgments that natural feelings and inclinations such as compassion and love lack. Therefore, the moral feeling of respect is the "basis" of other duties. As such, it can be connected and unified with other feelings such as love and compassion to extend its motivating power toward other persons by means of friendship.

(iii) Emotion Thesis: Since the moral feeling of respect is connected to the faculty of desire and the faculty of judgment, and since Kant conceives of the human will as both determinable by reason and sensibility, the moral agent feels her twofold determination at the same time as being opposed and in conflict. Due to the self-recognition and self-esteem as a moral being, the propensity of self-conceit that is based on the principle of sensibility is humiliated in moral judgment. This volitional process is expressed in terms of the feeling of the moral sublime and as a kind of pain that is due to one's self-recognition of self-conceit being outweighed by normative moral reasons.

(iv) Freedom Thesis: Since the human will is a unity of the lower and higher appetitive faculty, in feeling respect for the moral law the moral subject can be considered as autonomous from the perspective of pure practical reason and heteronomous from the perspective of inclinations. Kant's Freedom Thesis is related with the Emotion Thesis insofar in feeling moral respect the autonomous person feels her negative freedom as being independent from inclinations, and her positive freedom as being able to determine herself according to the moral law due to a causality of reason. Therefore, the Emotion Thesis is a phenomenological expression of Kant's Freedom Thesis.

(v) Subjectivity Thesis: Moral respect is volitional self-consciousness and self-approbation of pure practical reason within a finite rational *and* sensible being. In volitionally endorsing the universal law, and in recognizing one's autonomy, the moral law determines the will and brings about respect, which is intentionally directed to it. Since respect is causally related to the moral law as its effect, its reflection of the moral law is morality from a volitionally subjective point of view. In reflecting on the moral law and in incorporating it into one's maxim, the moral feeling of respect expresses morality subjectively. As such, the moral feeling of respect realizes the transition from mere legality to morality, which we can understand both in terms of normative and motivating reasons.

(vi) Intentionality Thesis: Insofar as moral respect is interpreted in terms of moral autonomy, it is originally directed toward the moral law, albeit not as something external, but as an *internal* affirmation and moral self-approbation in terms of a practical judgment. The moral feeling of respect is primarily self-respect, however not as an individual but as an individual being that is subject to the moral law. By self-reflectively endorsing one's being subject to the moral law, one realizes one's moral autonomy and proceeds from legality to morality.

(vii) Normativity Thesis: Respect is the very condition of having and recognizing duties, because self-respect is the necessary condition for being *susceptible* to duties that concern other persons. As such, respect is closely connected to conscience, which is also one of the four "*subjective* conditions of receptiveness to the concept of duty" (6:399). However, conscience is not directly related to moral autonomy, as moral respect is. Rather conscience is indirectly related to autonomy – not through the law-giving of reason, which concerns the will, but through reason's *judging itself* (6:186). Since the moral feeling of respect enables the transition from legality to morality, as Kant argues, it is the susceptibility and basis of duties, because only that way they become visible in terms of morality as subjective forms of autonomy and not merely of external legality. Since we are responsible for cultivating our susceptibility to moral respect for moral motivation, it follows that the moral feeling of respect is not sufficient for moral action but rather demands our faculty of choice. Therefore, electivism about respect needs to be understood in terms of cultivism to allow for moral imputability in moral motivation.

References

Citations of Kant's works refer to the volume and page number of the Academy Edition of Immanuel Kant, *Gesammelte Schriften* (Berlin: Walter de Gruyter and predecessors, 1900–). Translations are based on the Cambridge Edition of the Works of Immanuel Kant, general eds. Paul Guyer and Allen Wood (Cambridge: Cambridge University Press, 1992). Translations other than from the Cambridge Edition are mine.

Allison, Henry (1983). *Kant's Transcendental Idealism: An Interpretation and Defense*, New Haven: Yale University Press.

Allison, Henry (1990). *Kant's Theory of Freedom*, Cambridge: Cambridge University Press.

Alvarez, Maria and Way, Jonathan (2024). Reasons for Action: Justification, Motivation, Explanation. In Edward N. Zalta and Uri Nodelman (eds.), *The Stanford Encyclopedia of Philosophy*, https://plato.stanford.edu/archives/fall2024/entries/reasons-just-vs-expl.

Ameriks, Karl (2010). Reality, Reason, and Religion in the Development of Kant's Ethics. In Benjamin James Bruxvoort Lipscomb and James Krueger (eds.), *Kant's Moral Metaphysics*, Berlin: De Gruyter, 23–47.

Ameriks, Karl (2013). Vindicating Autonomy. In Oliver Sensen (ed.), *Kant on Moral Autonomy*, Cambridge: Cambridge University Press, 53–70.

Bagnoli, Carla (2003). Respect and Loving Attention. *Canadian Journal of Philosophy*, 33(4), 483–516.

Baron, Marcia W. (1997). Love and Respect in the Doctrine of Virtue. *The Southern Journal of Philosophy*, 36(Supplement), 29–44.

Baxley, Anne Margaret (2010). *Kant's Theory of Virtue: The Value of Autocracy*, Cambridge: Cambridge University Press.

Beck, Lewis White (1960). *A Commentary on Kant's Critique of Practical Reason*, Chicago: The University of Chicago Press.

Berg, Anastasia (2021). Kant on Moral Respect. *Archiv für Geschichte der Philosophie*, 103(4), 730–60.

Broadie, Alexander and Pybus, Elizabeth M. (1975). Kant's Concept of "Respect." *Kant-Studien*, 66(1), 58–64.

Buchheim, Thomas (2001). Die Universalität des Bösen nach Kants Religionsschrift. In Gerhard, Volker, Horstmann, Rolf-Peter and Schumacher, Ralph. (eds.), *Kant und die Berliner Aufklärung: Akten des IX. Internationalen Kant-Kongresses*, Berlin: De Gruyter, 652–61.

Cohen, Alix (ed.) (2014). *Kant on Emotion and Value*, London: Palgrave Macmillan.

Cohen, Alix (2017). Kant on the Moral Cultivation of Feelings. In Alix Cohen and Robert Stern (eds.), *Thinking about the Emotions: A Philosophical History*, Oxford: Oxford University Press, 172–83.

Cohen, Alix (2018). Rational Feelings. In Kelly Sorensen and Diane Williamson (eds.), *Kant and the Faculty of Feeling*, Cambridge: Cambridge University Press, 9–24.

Cohen, Alix (2020). A Kantian Account of Emotions as Feelings. *Mind*, 129-(514), 429–60.

DeWitt, Janelle (2014). Respect for the Moral Law: The Emotional Side of Reason. *Philosophy*, 89, 31–62.

Dillon, Robin S. (2022). Respect. In Edward N. Zalta and Uri Nodelman (eds.), *The Stanford Encyclopedia of Philosophy*, https://plato.stanford.edu/archives/fall2022/entries/respect.

Drummond, John J. (2006). Respect as a Moral Emotion: A Phenomenological Approach. *Husserl Studies*, 22, 1–27.

Engstrom, Steven (2010). The *Triebfeder* of Pure Practical Reason. In Andrews Reath and Jens Timmermann (eds.), *Kant's Critique of Practical Reason. A Critical Guide*, Cambridge: Cambridge University Press, 90–118.

Frankfurt, Harry G. (1994). Autonomy, Necessity and Love. In Hans Friedrich Fulda and Rolf-Peter Horstmann (eds.), *Vernunftbegriffe in der Moderne: Stuttgarter Hegel-Kongress 1993*, Stuttgart: Klett-Cotta, 433–47.

Frierson, Patrick (2010). Two Standpoints and the Problem of Moral Anthropology. In Benjamin James Bruxvoort Lipscomb and James K. Krueger (eds.), *Kant's Moral Metaphysics*, Berlin: De Gruyter, 83–110.

Frierson, Patrick (2014). *Kant's Empirical Psychology*, Cambridge: Cambridge University Press.

Geiger, Ido (2011). Rational Feelings and Moral Agency. *Kantian Review*, 16(2), 283–308.

Goy, Ina (2010). Immanuel Kant on the Moral Feeling of Respect. In Pablo Muchnik (ed.), *Rethinking Kant Volume 2*, Newcastle: Cambridge Scholars, 156–79.

Grenberg, Jeanine (2011). Making Sense of the Relationship of Reason and Sensibility in Kant's Ethics. *Kantian Review*, 16(3), 461–72.

Grenberg, Jeanine (2013). *Kant's Defense of Common Moral Experience: A Phenomenological Account*, Cambridge: Cambridge University Press.

Guevara, Daniel (2000). *Kant's Theory of Moral Motivation*, Boulder: Westview Press.

Guyer, Paul (2012). Schopenhauer, Kant and Compassion. *Kantian Review*, 17(3), 403–29.

Guyer, Paul (2016). Kant on Moral Feelings: From the Lectures to the Metaphysics of Morals. In Paul Guyer (ed.), *The Virtues of Freedom: Selected Essays on Kant*, Oxford: Oxford University Press, 235–59.

Guyer, Paul (2018). Moral Worth and Moral Motivation: Kant's Real View. In Dina Emundts and Sally Sedgwick (eds.), *Internationales Jahrbuch des Deutschen Idealismus / International Yearbook of German Idealism* 13 (2015), *Begehren / Desire*, Berlin: De Gruyter, 19–37.

Helm, Bennett (2021). Love. In Edward N. Zalta (ed.), *The Stanford Encyclopedia of Philosophy*, https://plato.stanford.edu/archives/fall2021/entries/love.

Henrich, Dieter (1994). Ethics of Autonomy. In Richard L. Velkley (ed.), *The Unity of Reason: Essays on Kant's Philosophy*, Cambridge, MA: Harvard University Press, 89–121.

Henrich, Dieter (2009). Hutcheson and Kant. In Karl Ameriks and Otfried Höffe (eds.), *Kant's Legal and Moral Philosophy*, Cambridge: Cambridge University Press, 29–57.

Herrera, Larry (2000). Kant on the Moral *Triebfeder*. *Kant-Studien*, 91(4), 395–410.

Hutcheson, Francis (2004). *An Inquiry into the Original of Our Ideas of Beauty and Virtue in Two Treatises* (1725), ed. and with an introduction by Wolfgang Leidhold, Indianapolis: Liberty Fund.

Klemme, Heiner F. (2006). Praktische Gründe und moralische Motivation: Eine deontologische Perspektive. In Heiner F. Klemme, Manfred Kühn, and Dieter Schönecker (eds.), *Moralische Motivation: Kant und die Alternativen*, Hamburg: Meiner, 113–53.

Klemme, Heiner F. (2007). Motivational Internalism: A Kantian Perspective on Moral Motives and Reasons. In Gábor Boros, Herman de Dijn and Martin Moors (eds.), *The Concept of Love in 17th and 18th Century Philosophy*, Leuven: Leuven University Press, 227–44.

Kolomý, Vojtěch (2023). Kant on Moral Feeling and Respect. *Kantian Review*, 28(1), 105–23.

Kriegel, Uriah and Timmons, Mark (2021). The Phenomenology of Kantian Respect for Persons. In Richard Dean and Oliver Sensen (eds.), *Respect: Philosophical Essays*, New York: Oxford University Press, 77–98.

Lauener, Henri (1981). Der systematische Stellenwert des Gefühls der Achtung in Kants Ethik. *Dialectica*, 35(1), 243–64.

Lipscomb, Benjamin (2010). Moral Imperfection and Moral Phenomenology in Kant. In Benjamin James Bruxvoort Lipscomb and James Krueger (eds.), *Kant's Moral Metaphysics*, Berlin: De Gruyter, 49–79.

MacBeath, A. Murray (1973). Kant on Moral Feeling. *Kant-Studien*, 64(3), 283–314.

Maimon, Salomon (1791). *Philosophisches Wörterbuch oder Beleuchtung der wichtigsten Gegenstände der Philosophie, in alphabetischer Ordnung*, Berlin: Unger.

McCarty, Richard (1993). Moral Motivation and the Feeling of Respect. *Journal of the History of Philosophy*, 31(3), 421–35.

McCarty, Richard (1994). *Motivation and Moral Choice in Kant's Theory of Rational Agency*. Kant-Studien, 85(1), 15–31.

McCarty, Richard (2009). *Kant's Theory of Action*, Oxford: Oxford University Press.

Merritt, Melissa M. (2018). *The Sublime*, Cambridge: Cambridge University Press.

Metz, Wilhelm (2004). Das Gefühl der Achtung in Kants Kritik der praktischen Vernunft. In Gerhard Schönrich (ed.), *Normativität und Faktizität: Skeptische und transzendentalphilosophische Positionen im Anschluß an Kant*, Dresden: Thelem, 141–50.

Moran, Kate (2014). Delusions of Virtue: Kant on Self-Conceit. *Kantian Review*, 19(3), 419–47.

Noller, Jörg (2016). *Die Bestimmung des Willens: Zum Problem individueller Freiheit im Ausgang von Kant*, 2nd ed., Freiburg: Alber.

Noller, Jörg (2019). Reason's Feeling: A Systematic Reconstruction of Kant's Theory of Moral Respect. *SATS – Northern European Journal of Philosophy*, 20(1), 1–18.

Noller, Jörg (2021). The Logic of Illusion: Kant on the Reasons of Error. *Theoria*, 87(6), 1468–80.

Noller, Jörg (2022). Rationalizing: Kant on Moral Self-deception. *SATS – Northern European Journal of Philosophy*, 23(2), 175–89.

Noller, Jörg (2023). Obscuring Reason: Kant and Fichte on Acting against the Moral Law. *History of Philosophy Quarterly*, 40(4), 302–16.

Noller, Jörg (2024). *The Fate of Choice: Freedom and Imputabiliy in Kant and his Early Successors*, Leiden: Brill.

Noller, Jörg and Walsh, John (eds.) (2022). *Kant's Early Critics on Freedom of the Will*, Cambridge: Cambridge University Press.

Papish, Laura (2018). *Kant on Evil, Self-Deception, and Moral Reform*, Oxford: Oxford University Press.

Reath, Andrews (1989). Kant's Theory of Moral Sensibility: Respect for the Moral Law and the Influence of Inclination. *Kant-Studien*, 80(3), 284–302.

Reath, Andrews (2006). Hedonism, Heteronomy, and Kant's Principle of Happiness. In Andrews Reath (ed.), *Agency and Autonomy in Kant's Moral Theory*, Oxford: Oxford University Press, 33–66.

Reath, Andreas (2013). Kant's Conception of Autonomy of the Will. In Oliver Sensen (ed.), *Kant on Moral Autonomy*, Cambridge: Cambridge University Press, 32–52.

Rosati, Connie S. (2016). Moral Motivation. In Edward N. Zalta (ed.), *The Stanford Encyclopedia of Philosophy*, https://plato.stanford.edu/archives/win2016/entries/moral-motivation.

Scarantino, Andrea and Ronald de Sousa (2021). Emotion. In Edward N. Zalta (ed.), *The Stanford Encyclopedia of Philosophy*, https://plato.stanford.edu/archives/sum2021/entries/emotion.

Schadow, Steffi (2013). *Achtung für das Gesetz: Moral und Motivation bei Kant*, Berlin: De Gruyter.

Schmid, Carl Christian Erhard (1790). *Versuch einer Moralphilosophie*, Jena: Cröker.

Sensen, Oliver (2013a). Duties to Others From Respect (TL 6:462 – 468). In Andreas Trampota, Oliver Sensen, and Jens Timmermann (eds.), *Kant's "Tugendlehre": A Comprehensive Commentary*, Berlin: De Gruyter, 343–63.

Sensen, Oliver (2013b). The Moral Importance of Autonomy. In Oliver Sensen (ed.), *Kant on Moral Autonomy*, Cambridge: Cambridge University Press, 262–81.

Shaftesbury, Anthony Ashley Cooper, Third Earl of (2000). *Characteristics of Men, Manners, Opinions, Times* (1711), Cambridge: Cambridge University Press.

Singleton, Jane (2007). Kant's Account of Respect: A Bridge between Rationality and Anthropology. *Kantian Review*, 12(1), 40–60.

Sorensen, Kelly and Williamson, Diane (eds.) (2018). *Kant and the Faculty of Feeling*, Cambridge: Cambridge University Press.

Sticker, Martin (2021). *Rationalizing (Vernünfteln)*, Cambridge: Cambridge University Press.

Sytsma, Sharon E. (1993). The Role of *Achtung* in Kant's Moral Theory. *Auslegung*, 19(1), 117–22.

Theis, Robert (2005). Respect de la loi, respect de la personne: Kant. *Revue Philosophique de Louvain*, 103(3), 331–46.

Timmermann, Jens (2003). *Sittengesetz und Freiheit: Untersuchungen zu Immanuel Kants Theorie des freien Willens*, Berlin: De Gruyter.

Timmermann, Jens (2022). *Kant's Will at the Crossroads: An Essay on the Failings of Practical Rationality*, Oxford: Oxford University Press.

Walschots, Michael (2017). Hutcheson and Kant: Moral Sense and Moral Feeling. In Elizabeth Robinson and Chris W. Surprenant (eds.), *Kant and the Scottish Enlightenment*, London: Routledge, 36–54.

Walschots, Michael (2022). *Achtung* in Kant and Smith. *Kant-Studien*, 113(2), 238–68.

Walschots, Michael (2024). Incentives of the Mind: Kant and Baumgarten on the Impelling Causes of Desire. *Archiv für Geschichte der Philosophie*, aop, 1–27.

Ware, Owen (2014). Kant on Moral Sensibility and Moral Motivation. *Journal of the History of Philosophy*, 52(4), 727–46.

Ware, Owen (2015). Accessing the Moral Law through Feeling. *Kantian Review*, 20(2), 301–11.

Ware, Owen (2019). The Duty of Self-Knowledge. *Philosophy and Phenomenological Research*, 79(3), 671–98.

Watkins, Eric (2005). *Kant and the Metaphysics of Causality*, Cambridge: Cambridge University Press.

Wood, Allen (2010). Respect and Recognition. In John Skorupski (ed.), *The Routledge Companion to Ethics*, London: Routledge: 562–72.

Zinkin, Melissa (2006). Respect for the Law and the Use of Dynamical Terms in Kant's Theory of Moral Motivation. *Archiv für Geschichte der Philosophie*, 88(1), 31–53.

Acknowledgements

I would like to thank the anonymous reviewers of this Element for their helpful remarks.

Cambridge Elements

The Philosophy of Immanuel Kant

Desmond Hogan
Princeton University

Desmond Hogan joined the philosophy department at Princeton in 2004. His interests include Kant, Leibniz and German rationalism, early modern philosophy, and questions about causation and freedom. Recent work includes 'Kant on the Foreknowledge of Contingent Truths', *Res Philosophica* 91(1) (2014); 'Kant's Theory of Divine and Secondary Causation', in Brandon Look (ed.) *Leibniz and Kant*, Oxford University Press (2021); 'Kant and the Character of Mathematical Inference', in Carl Posy and Ofra Rechter (eds.) *Kant's Philosophy of Mathematics Vol. I*, Cambridge University Press (2020).

Howard Williams
University of Cardiff

Howard Williams was appointed Honorary Distinguished Professor at the Department of Politics and International Relations, University of Cardiff in 2014. He is also Emeritus Professor in Political Theory at the Department of International Politics, Aberystwyth University, a member of the Coleg Cymraeg Cenedlaethol (Welsh-language national college) and a Fellow of the Learned Society of Wales. He is the author of *Marx* (1980); *Kant's Political Philosophy* (1983); *Concepts of Ideology* (1988); *Hegel, Heraclitus and Marx's Dialectic* (1989); *International Relations in Political Theory* (1992); *International Relations and the Limits of Political Theory* (1996); *Kant's Critique of Hobbes: Sovereignty and Cosmopolitanism* (2003); *Kant and the End of War* (2012) and is currently editor of the journal Kantian Review. He is writing a book on the Kantian legacy in political philosophy for a new series edited by Paul Guyer.

Allen Wood
Indiana University

Allen Wood is Ward W. and Priscilla B. Woods Professor Emeritus at Stanford University. He was a John S. Guggenheim Fellow at the Free University in Berlin, a National Endowment for the Humanities Fellow at the University of Bonn and Isaiah Berlin Visiting Professor at the University of Oxford. He is on the editorial board of eight philosophy journals, five book series and The Stanford Encyclopedia of Philosophy. Along with Paul Guyer, Professor Wood is co-editor of The Cambridge Edition of the Works of Immanuel Kant and translator of the Critique of Pure Reason. He is the author or editor of a number of other works, mainly on Kant, Hegel and Karl Marx. His most recently published books are *Fichte's Ethical Thought*, Oxford University Press (2016) and *Kant and Religion*, Cambridge University Press (2020). Wood is a member of the American Academy of Arts and Sciences.

About the Series

This Cambridge Elements series provides an extensive overview of Kant's philosophy and its impact upon philosophy and philosophers. Distinguished Kant specialists provide an up-to-date summary of the results of current research in their fields and give their own take on what they believe are the most significant debates influencing research, drawing original conclusions.

Cambridge Elements

The Philosophy of Immanuel Kant

Elements in the Series

Kant on Self-Control
Marijana Vujošević

Kant on Rational Sympathy
Benjamin Vilhauer

The Moral Foundation of Right
Paul Guyer

The Postulate of Public Right
Patrick Capps and Julian Rivers

Kant on the History and Development of Practical Reason
Olga Lenczewska

Kant's Ideas of Reason
Katharina T. Kraus

Kant on Marriage
Charlotte Sabourin

Kant and Teleology
Thomas Teufel

Kant on Social Suffering
Nuria Sánchez Madrid

Kant's Natural Philosophy
Marius Stan

Kant Incorporated
Garrath Williams

Kant on Respect (Achtung)
Jörg Noller

A full series listing is available at: www.cambridge.org/EPIK

Printed by Integrated Books International,
United States of America